ROBIN SMITH-JOHNSON

CAPE COD
CURIOSITIES

JEREMIAH'S GUTTER

The Historian Who Flew as Santa

PUKWUDGIES

— *and* MORE —

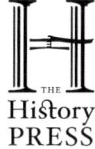

THE
History
PRESS

Published by The History Press
Charleston, SC
www.historypress.com

Copyright © 2018 by Robin Smith-Johnson
All rights reserved

Front cover: Image of pukwudgie drawn by Sarah Haynes.

First published 2018

Manufactured in the United States

ISBN 9781467138581

Library of Congress Control Number: 2017963915

For my family—for all your love, support and patience during the writing of this book.

CONTENTS

Contents

ACKNOWLEDGEMENTS

This book has been a labor of love, and I could not have done it without the help of libraries and individuals on Cape Cod.

First, I would like to thank Rebekah Ambrose-Dalton, special collections librarian and archivist in the W.B. Nickerson Room at Cape Cod Community College. She was kind enough to help me pick out photographs for this volume. I would also like to thank Jean Young of the Chatham Historical Society for finding period photos of Joseph C. Lincoln as part of my research. I am also deeply appreciative for help from area libraries, including Cotuit, Mashpee and Sturgis libraries.

I wish to thank Paul Pronovost, editor of the *Cape Cod Times*, for permission to use *Times* photos. Ritchie Kolnos, IT specialist at the *Cape Cod Times*, was instrumental in helping me with my photos as well. I would also like to thank *Times* photographer, Merrily Cassidy, for the author photo.

I would like to thank my mother, Muriel Smith, for sharing the postcard collection from the estate of my late father, Wendell Everett Smith, an antiquarian book dealer. I'm grateful to Gregory R. Johnson and Cynthia Sherrick Mitchell for contributing photos to this collection. I also want to thank my sister, Laurie Smith Murphy, for sharing her recollections of the 1973 Nauset Beach riptide disaster.

I'm indebted to Barbara Clark for help in editing my book, as well as Devin Wells Johnson for a careful reading of the manuscript. I also wish to thank Gwenn Friss and Susan Eastman of the *Cape Cod Times* for their support and friendship.

ACKNOWLEDGEMENTS

I would like to thank the wonderful folks at The History Press: Lia Grabowski, acquisitions editor, for bringing me onboard with this project, Chad Rhoad, senior acquisitions editor, and Ryan Finn, senior project editor, for keeping me on track with my manuscript.

I would like to thank my family for their uncomplaining support. It has been a wonderful journey of historical research and exploration.

INTRODUCTION

Cape Cod is a unique, beautiful and sometimes curious place. What is meant by "curious"? To be curious means not only to discover something strange or unusual, but also to have the desire to learn about something—to want to know more. It is in this spirit, the spirit of exploration, that these stories have been compiled to entice and entertain the reader.

There are stories about famous people, from the notorious Tony Costa murders to the homey chronicles of Joseph Lincoln; famous places, like the Sandwich Glass Museum and the Chatham Marconi Station; and fantastical stories about the Pukwudgies and the elusive Marsh People. Old books, news articles and microfilm have fleshed out this investigation.

The Cape offers strange and surprising tales, from a 1973 riptide disaster at Nauset Beach in Orleans to the presence of a lonely ghost boy at the Hyannis Public Library. The old saying that truth is stranger than fiction often applies to these narratives. Irish novelist Laurence Sterne once wrote, "What a large volume of adventures may be grasped within the span of his little life by him who interests his heart in everything."

Digging up the past is a joy and sometimes an obsession. Stories call out demanding to be told. Come walk the byways and winding lanes of this quaint and dynamic place. There is so much to experience and treasure in this place by the sea.

THE CREATION OF THE CAPE COD CANAL

The Cape Cod Canal is a man-made waterway that connects Cape Cod to the mainland, but for Cape Codders, the canal is so much more. It is the first thing visitors see when they arrive at their vacation destination. For locals, the experience of seeing the bridges and the glimmering waters of the canalway serves as the symbolic entrance to Cape Cod.

Did you know that it took 317 years for the Cape Cod Canal to become a reality? Myles Standish envisioned a canal across the narrow neck of land joining Cape Cod to the mainland. Before the canal was built, ships and schooners had to navigate around the Cape, with its treacherous access to the Atlantic Ocean. A canal was seen as being a practical solution.

In 1862, it was proposed that the canal be built at sea level, instead of implementing earlier plans that called for a lock canal. Then, in 1880, a group called the Cape Cod Canal Company was granted a charter to begin digging. At first, the five hundred workers brought in for the job tried to dig with shovels and wheelbarrows. Later, F.A. Lockwood constructed a huge dredge to supplement the workers' efforts. However, the project was ultimately abandoned because it was costly and the digging methods ineffective.

In 1899, a new charter was granted, and the work was headed by New York financier August Belmont. On March 27, 1907, the Boston, Cape Cod and New York Canal Company entered into a contract with the Cape

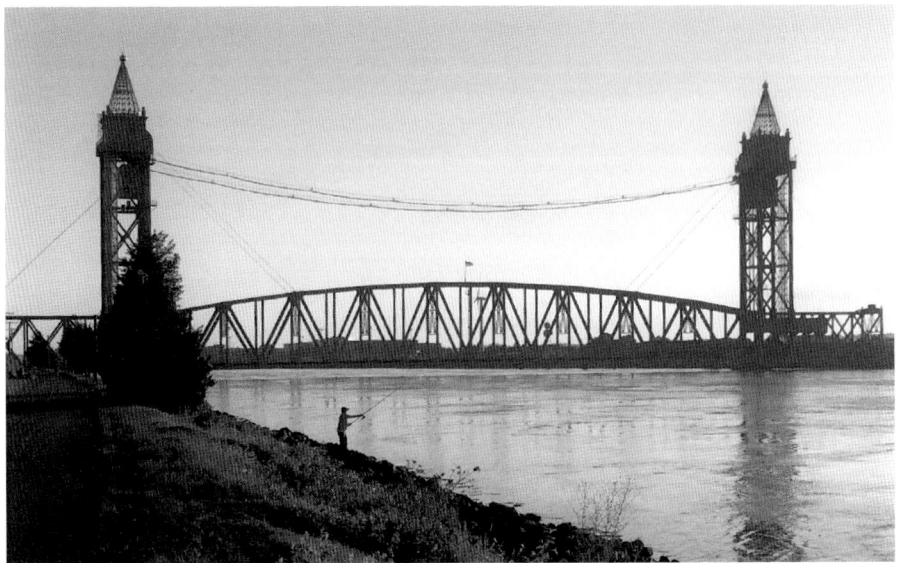

The Railroad Bridge spanning the Cape Cod Canal. *Courtesy of the* Cape Cod Times.

Cod Construction Company. Work finally began on June 19, 1909, using much more modern equipment. The canal opened five years later on July 29, 1914. The project cost $16.1 million. Initially, the canal was opened for sailing vessels of limited draft, with the full depth of twenty-five feet reached in 1918. The owners charged each passing vessel for use of the canal.

The Federal Railroad Administration took over the canal during World War I. When it tried to return it after the war was over, the original owners refused the deal. Then, on March 31, 1928, the federal government agreed to pay $11.5 million for the canal. The canal has operated as a toll-free waterway ever since. Later, the channel was widened in 1932 and 1935. The first Bourne Bridge was built between 1910 and 1913 and was later replaced with the present bridge in 1935. The Sagamore Bridge also opened in 1935; it originally was built as a drawbridge before the canal was widened. The Railroad Bridge, a vertical-lift bridge, carries railroad traffic across the canal. Construction started in 1935, and the bridge officially opened on December 29, 1935.

The canal itself opened on a limited basis in 1914 and was completed in 1916. It was widened and deepened, and by 1940, the Cape Cod Canal was the widest sea-level canal in the world. According to the U.S. Army Corps of Engineers' website, ship traffic can safely transit the waterway, and now more than twenty thousand vessels of all types use the canal annually.

A 1983 *Cape Cod Times* interview with a retired surveyor, Robert Waite, gave a first-person account of traveling over the Cape Cod Canal. During the 1918 flu epidemic, Waite's school in Wollaston closed for three weeks. Fourteen-year-old Waite and his friend Bill Edward rode their bicycles to visit Bill's grandparents in Chatham. He said, "We came down the old Route 3 that wove in and out of all the towns on the way. There was a wooden bridge over the Cape Cod Canal then. It had streetcar tracks on it for the Brockton-to-Hyannis trolley. As I remember, the bridge rolled back on tracks to let tall boats through. The Canal was more like a big ditch then." After the U.S. government purchased the canal in 1928, it was deepened and widened. The wooden bridge was replaced by steel structures, one at each end.

Tale of a 1937 Canal Passage

My mother told a fascinating story she remembered from childhood on her traveling through the Cape Cod Canal in 1937 at the age of ten. This was an interesting tidbit and something I had never heard about before. She grew up in Morristown, New Jersey, and took a trip with her mother, aunt and best friend in the summer of 1937. They traveled via cruise ship from New York to Boston and then traveled north by car to Maine. I did a quick internet search and found two cruise lines that might have been ones my mother traveled on: the old Fall River line and the Eastern Steamship *Acadia*. Although the *Acadia* traveled to Yarmouth, Nova Scotia, from New York, it could easily have stopped in Boston for a layover.

The trip from New York City to Boston was a two-day affair, so the little girls slept over on the boat. My mother remembers waking around 5:00 a.m. as they made the trip through the Cape Cod Canal. Since the canal bridges had only recently opened, this was a big event for Cape Codders, as well as two excited little girls. My mom said there were cars lining the Cape side of the canal, and they all had their headlights on as the big ship passed through. The girls stood on the deck and waved to all the well-wishers. The cars tooted back in response.

Now, summer visitors and Cape residents alike use the bridges on a daily basis. The existence of the canal also technically makes the Cape an island. Most visitors look forward to rounding a curve in the highway and seeing the arc of one of the bridges coming into view. It's both a comforting and beckoning view because it tells the weary traveler that he or she is almost home.

CAPE COD TRANSPORTATION

THEN AND NOW

THE HISTORY OF RAILROAD TRAVEL ON CAPE COD

Nowadays, the only trains on Cape Cod are Cape Cod Central Railroad's Dinner Train and the CapeFlyer train that runs from Boston to Cape Cod on summer weekends. However, the Cape has a long history of train travel. The railroad/shipping enterprise began in 1848. Before the railroad, transportation on the Cape consisted of horseback and wagons. The Old Colony Railroad line originated in Middleboro and made its way south to Hyannis on July 8, 1854. The wharf where the single line of track ended was one thousand feet long and two hundred feet wide. The first ship to meet up with the train was the *Nebraska* (from Nantucket). In the railroad's heyday, six schooners could be accommodated along the wharf as they waited to offload their cargo of both freight and passengers. Businesses sprouted up in the area. Some of the freight included lumber, grain, fish, coal, whale oil, agriculture (including cranberries) and building materials.

The Woods Hole tracks were finished in 1872, with the *Island Home* one of the first ships to stop there. While the Hyannis and Provincetown wharves featured single tracks (in Hyannis, this was a double track that merged into a single track to facilitate the picking up of passengers), the Woods Hole wharf had twelve tracks. It was surmised that a large fertilizer factory in Woods Hole was one institution that most needed the railroad for its shipping interests. The original wooden station was

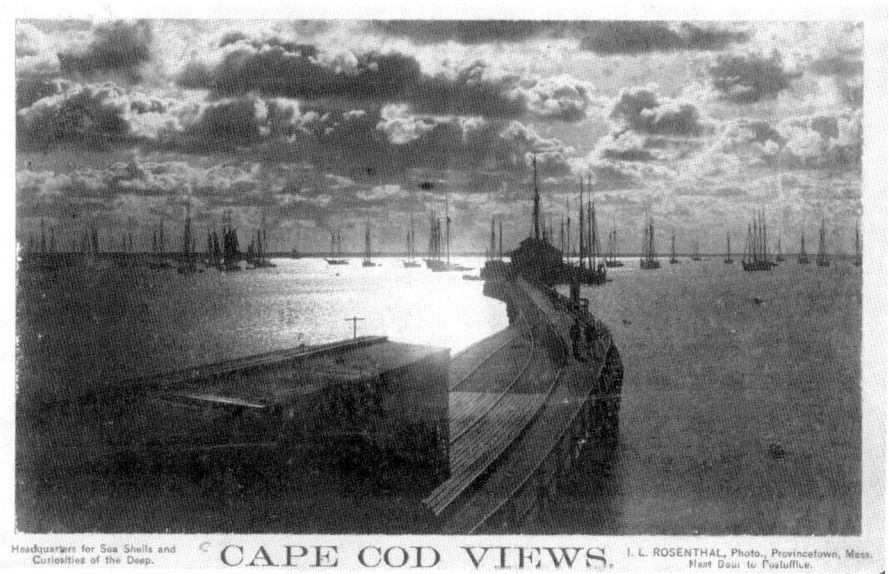

An old-fashioned postcard depicting a local railroad pier. *Courtesy of the W.B. Nickerson Archives, Cape Cod Community College.*

built at the end of the Woods Hole branch in 1872 and was replaced by a brick structure in 1899.

The Provincetown line was started in 1873 and, like the Hyannis wharf, had a single track. The wharf was on Harry Kemp Way, and the first train ran in July 1873. There were also smaller railroads on Martha's Vineyard and Nantucket designed to carry passengers, with most of the tracks made for lighter locomotives.

For locals and visitors alike, the train system opened up a faster, more reliable way to get around Cape Cod. Tourists could step on a train in New York City, make connections in Boston and arrive in Provincetown several hours later. Almost every Cape town had its own depot, and locals eagerly awaited the Boston train to bring major newspapers and mail. At the advent of both world wars, families said goodbye to their departing soldiers as they boarded trains to take them to off-Cape training camps and, ultimately, overseas.

Railroads began to decline in the 1900s with the introduction of cars and trucks. The Hyannis wharf, abandoned in 1930, was sold to private interests in 1938. In Provincetown, the last rail car ran in 1919, and the wharf was sold to the town in 1928. The passenger rails ended in the 1950s, and now many of the old tracks have been taken out and replaced with bike paths.

CAPE AIR TRAVEL: A LOOK BACK

When the railroads were phased out in the 1950s, people began to look toward air travel. The Cape has never been without commercial airline service since the end of World War II.

In 1949, a young pilot named John Van Arsdale started the Provincetown-Boston Airlines to create service between those two terminals. Adults paid ten dollars to fly round trip, while kids flew for only five dollars. Unfortunately, the company was dogged by fatal accidents and financial burdens. The airline was taken over by the People Express in 1985.

A new era for Cape flight began in January 1987 with the announcement of a new airline: Cape Cod Air. Dan Wolf, the manager of the Chatham Municipal Airport and Cape Cod Aero Marine, presented plans for flights to Nantucket and Boston from Chatham. The airline was designed for tourists who wanted to reach Nantucket without fighting traffic to get a ferry to the island. Then, in 1989, Cape Cod Air took over air routes between Provincetown and Boston. At thirty years old, Dan Wolf became the president of Cape Air with his own office at Provincetown Airport and backup at Barnstable Municipal Airport.

In 1990, Cape Air expanded its commuter airline operation when it took over Hyannis–Martha's Vineyard flights from Edgartown Air Inc. Plans were afoot to fly nine-passenger Cessna 402 twin-engine airplanes. Twenty years ago, a round trip ticket cost sixty-two dollars. In 1993, Hyannis-based Cape Air expanded its commuter air service into Florida with flights between Key West and Naples. The young airline's motto was "Make our customers happy and have a good time doing it."

Near accidents marred Cape Air's perfect safety record. Smoke in the cockpit forced the return of a Cape Air flight bound for Nantucket back to Barnstable Municipal Airport in December 1999. The pilot, Thomas Shanahan, touched down safely, and the nine passengers were transferred to another flight. In June 2000, passengers described panic aboard a Cape Air plane in an aborted, roller coaster flight to the Vineyard. The plane was forced to return to Barnstable. No one was hurt, but the rough landing caused one of the tires to burst.

Other accidents happened in 2001, such as when a flight from Provincetown to Martha's Vineyard crashed on approach to the airport. The pilot and sole passenger escaped with injuries before the plane burst into flames. In that same year, a twenty-nine-year-old pilot, Jason Watson of Mashpee, suffered second-degree burns on his legs when his plane crashed and burned shortly after takeoff on a Logan to Nantucket flight.

Finally, in April 2009, Cape Air announced another new route that would connect Westchester County, New York, with Martha's Vineyard and Nantucket. Later, the airline added a number of new routes around the Northeast.

It's nice to know that we're not cut off from the mainland. We can hop on a plane and escape to the wider world. Air travel to and from Cape Cod has truly come of age.

A CAPE COD AIR TRAGEDY

A routine flight turned deadly on June 17, 1979, when Air New England Flight 248 went down in Yarmouth Port. Ten people were aboard the plane, and all survived except the pilot, George Parmenter, sixty, of Centerville, who was killed instantly. Parmenter was a senior pilot for Air New England and one of the company's co-founders. The plane, an eighteen-seat De Havilland Twin Otter (registered N383EX), crashed around 11:00 p.m. It was heading to Barnstable Municipal Airport from New York's LaGuardia Airport before it disappeared into the woods of the three-hundred-acre Camp Greenough, about one and a half miles northeast of the airport.

The passengers were bruised, covered in fuel and disoriented. An eighteen-year-old girl, Suzanne Mourad, was able to stumble through the woods and make her way to Route 6. She flagged down a car, which took her to the nearby airport. At that point, family members had gathered, but airport officials had little information about the crash. Suzanne was able to show them to the crash site. In a *Cape Cod Times* article written thirty years after the crash, she was quoted as saying, "What stands out to all of us is once we got out of the plane, we kept looking for the helicopters and looking for the bright lights and listening for the sirens and there was no noise. What specifically I think all of us remember is like, 'Oh, my God,' you know, 'Where is everybody?'"

According to a National Transportation Safety accident report, the crash occurred during an instrument landing system (ILS) approach and was due to pilot error. The report stated, "Of the eight passengers and a crew of two aboard, the captain was killed, the first officer and six passengers were injured severely and two passengers received minor injuries. The aircraft was

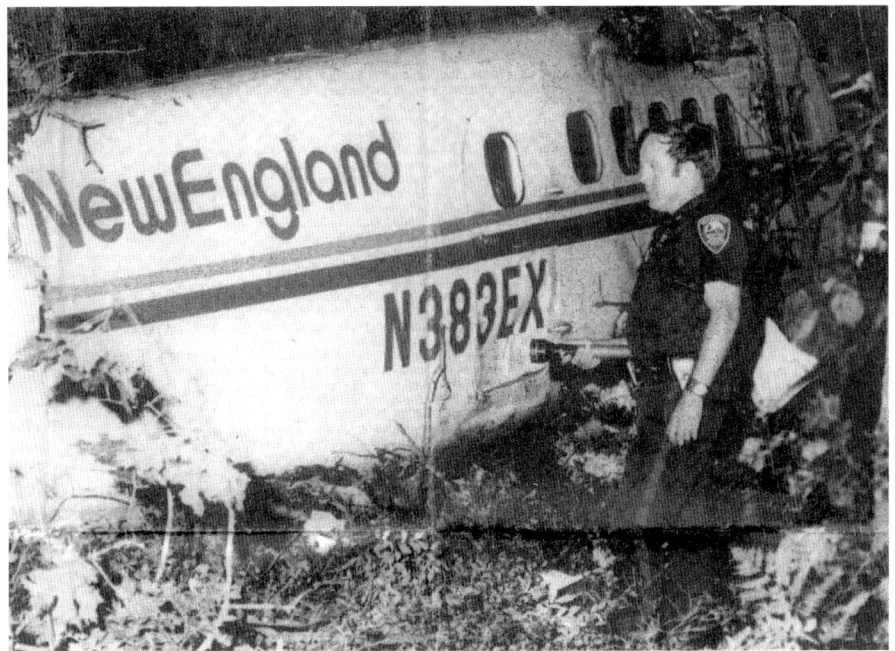

The New England *N383EX*, a downed plane, circa 1979. *Courtesy of the* Cape Cod Times.

destroyed." There was some speculation that the pilot was either physically or psychologically impaired. He did not respond to routine callouts. In addition, Captain Parmenter wore glasses, but the glasses were found in the cockpit in their carrying case. The weather may also have contributed to the crash since there was fog and drizzle in the vicinity and reduced visibility.

Passengers escaped through one of the cabin's main doors after they tried unsuccessfully to get the emergency exits to work. They were desperate to get off the plane because of the threat of fire and the strong smell of fuel. A medical student onboard checked on the other passengers, and the two most seriously injured were carried out of the plane.

One of the passengers, Robert Sabbag, later wrote a book about his experience titled *Down Around Midnight: A Memoir of Crash and Survival.* According to a *New York Post* review, "The best passages are the recreation of the event itself which, like all air crashes, thrill and horrify through sheer physics. Just before it crashed the plane descended at 1,500 feet a minute and the G-force was sufficient to explode the links on the author's watch." In an interesting twist, a young Ted Kennedy was on the flight just before the one that crashed.

TRAGEDY AT SEA

THE STEAMER PORTLAND

On November 27, 1898, the steamer *Portland* was lost with all on board. The official passenger list went down with the ship, so the exact number of fatalities is unknown, but between 176 and 191 people died in that disaster. The *Portland* left India Wharf in Boston, at 7:00 p.m. Saturday night on November 26 on its regular run to Portland, Maine. The ship was a wooden-hulled side-wheeler that measured 281 feet long and was built in Bath in 1890. A fierce storm began in midafternoon on that Saturday after Thanksgiving, and by midnight, it was a howling blizzard. The snow continued to fall through Sunday. Hurricane-force winds were believed to have reached ninety miles per hour. The ship was last spotted about 1:00 a.m. Sunday off Gloucester by crew members of the *Maude S.*, which was headed to Boston. There were also reports that surf watchers off Provincetown saw it momentarily Sunday morning, tossing near Peaked Hill Bars during a lull in the storm.

According to a *Cape Cod Standard Times* article from November 26, 1959, "Experts theorize the vessel's captain, Hollis H. Blanchard, after realizing the magnitude of the storm, tried to get into the lee of the Cape, in Provincetown Harbor, but couldn't make it, and the ship foundered on the Peaked Hill Bars, off the back shore." The first sign that disaster had struck was debris coming ashore, including milk cans, barrels, chairs and mattresses. Two days

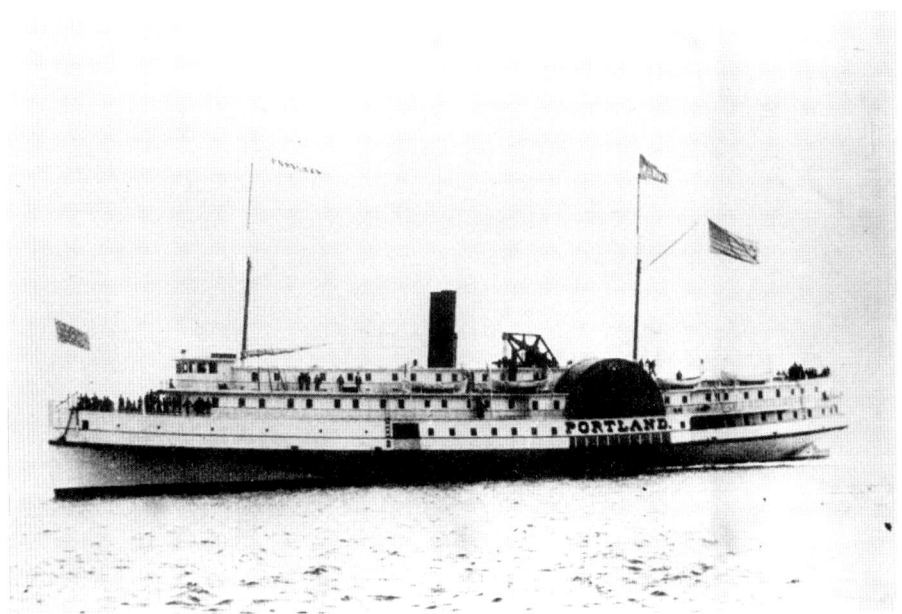

A black-and-white photo of the steamer *Portland. Courtesy of the* Cape Cod Times.

later, the shore was covered with wreckage, and about thirty-five bodies were recovered. Watches discovered on the bodies were stopped between 9:30 and 10:00 (it was unclear if the time was a.m. or p.m.). In the ensuing years, other wreckage would be found in fishermen's nets.

Since there were no survivors, we may never really know what happened. One theory is that the *Portland* rammed another vessel during the storm, possibly the *Patagoet*, a ship that left New York with seventeen aboard and was never heard from again. Another vessel the *Portland* could have collided with was the cargo schooner *Addie E. Snow* out of Seal Harbor, Maine. It has been estimated that 140 vessels sank during the Northeast storm.

In 1971, a *Boston Herald Traveler* article reported that "even before the coastal side-wheeler was launched, a fellow shipbuilder had a premonition that the steamer would sink off Cape Cod. And, nine years later, the Boston-to-Portland ship foundered at that precise spot." Over the years, divers have searched for remnants of the ship. There was an unsubstantiated story that there was $18,000 worth of uncut jewels in the ship's safe. In 2008, five Massachusetts scuba divers reached the remains of the *Portland*, sometimes called the "*Titanic* of New England." A plaque was dedicated outside Truro's Highland Light, displaying a picture of the steamer *Portland*.

Wreck of the *Jason*

Before the *Portland* went down off Race Point in 1898, there was another tragedy off the Outer Cape. On December 5, 1893, the *Jason*, a full-rigged British ship, struck a sandbar off the coast of Truro in a northeast gale. Only one of the twenty-six-person crew survived. This treacherous area is often called the "graveyard of ships," and countless lives and fishing vessels have been lost in its waters.

The *Jason* left Calcutta, India, ten months earlier bound for Boston. It carried ten thousand bales of jute headed for New England factories. It seemed a cursed voyage from the start. As it crossed the Indian Ocean, the ship's masts were torn off by a tornado, and the ship had to undergo repairs. Next, the ship endured bad weather near the Bahamas. The ship's captain had trouble making necessary calculations for the final leg of the trip due to fog and bad weather. In the end, the ship encountered heavy rain, sleet and snow. It was also observed to be dangerously close to land.

Lifesavers waited on shore because they could tell the *Jason* was in perilous danger. The ship struck sandbars off the coast of Truro, about half a mile north of the Pamet Life-Saving Station. When the mainmast toppled, the sailors aboard the doomed ship fell into the icy waters. The ship broke in half, with its cargo lost as well. The only survivor, Samuel J. Evans, was found on the beach after he was washed overboard. He was half frozen and wearing only his underwear.

In William Quinn's book *Shipwrecks Around Cape Cod*, he noted that "the bodies of 20 of the crew were found and because of the reported overcrowding in the cemetery in Truro, they were buried in the cemetery vault in Wellfleet. Total loss of ship and cargo was listed in the records as $119,420."

One interesting phenomenon witnessed during the fierce storm was the "slatting" or beating of the sails. The official report on the wreck noted that the distant sails sounded like "peals of thunder, and the crashing of blocks and chains as they were flung back and forth against the wire rigging and the iron foremast, sent out volumes of blazing sparks that seemed to some of the bystanders like signals of distress." In his book, Quinn wrote that the "wrecked ship sounded like peals of thunder above the roar of the surf."

A granite stone was erected in Wellfleet's Oakdale Cemetery during the 1976 bicentennial dedicated to the twenty-five crew members who perished that long-ago day in 1893.

ANDREA DORIA: AN ILL-FATED VOYAGE

On July 25, 1956, the Italian liner *Andrea Doria* collided with the Swedish passenger ship *Stockholm* off the New England coast late on a very foggy night and began sinking. As many as 51 people on this ship, as well as 5 crewmen on the Swedish ship, died. However, 1,660 passengers aboard the *Andrea Doria* were rescued, most by grabbing lifeboats and anything that would float. The horrific accident happened about forty-five miles south of Nantucket. Like the ill-fated *Titanic*, the *Andrea Doria* was also advertised as being "unsinkable." The luxury liner sank twelve hours after the *Stockholm* rammed its heavy bow into the *Andrea Doria*'s hull.

As recounted in a *Cape Cod Standard Times* article, eighteen-year-old Dun Gifford recalled the initial impact. He had been relaxing with other young people around 11:00 p.m. Shortly before impact, he looked out to sea and saw the bright lights of the *Stockholm*. All he could think was "what a crazy place to have a lighthouse." He was quoted as saying, "My most vivid recollection was the violence of the collision. There was this great tearing of

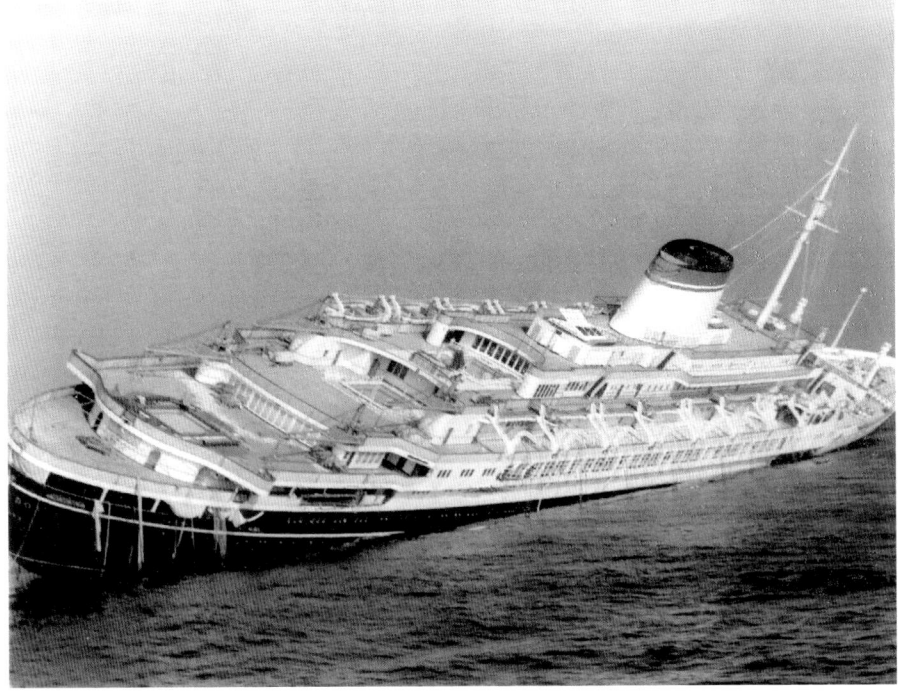

The sinking of the *Andrea Doria*, circa 1956. *Courtesy of the* Cape Cod Times.

metal and a shredding and wrenching noise as the two ships slid past each other." After he located his family, they waited hours to board a lifeboat. His father stayed behind, as only women and children were allowed to board the lifeboats. They were picked up by the *Ile de France*, a French liner, and one of several ships including the *Cape Ann* that arrived to pick up survivors. Dun's father was reunited with the family two hours after they arrived on the *Ile de France*. (Note: Gifford died in 2010 at the age of seventy-one.)

The injured passengers from both ships were brought to Nantucket. There, many were put on cargo planes and flown to Boston hospitals for treatment. The event incited a huge media response. The *New York Daily News* was the first newspaper to send a plane to Nantucket, followed by the *New York Times* and the *Chicago Tribune*.

In later years, the *Andrea Doria* became a lure for divers and explorers. In fact, it is sometimes called the "Mount Everest of Scuba Diving." In the years since the vessel sank in 220 feet of water, at least sixteen people have died while diving in the wreckage of the damaged ship looking for treasure. There were estimates of $2 million in currency, jewels, paintings and other artifacts still on board the ship. According to *Cape Cod Times* archives, the *Andrea Doria* was the last major transatlantic passenger vessel to sink before air transport became the preferred method of travel.

HAUNTED PLACES

Cape Cod is rich with stories and tales of haunted places. Many of the early settlers forged deep roots here and perhaps enjoy a satisfactory afterlife as well. Paranormal activity has been reported in cemeteries, inns, bed-and-breakfasts, restaurants and even outdoor locales. In a list put out by the Cape and Islands Paranormal Research Society (CAIPRS), there are entries such as Walking Train Track Ghost (apparition, mist) or Follins Pond (contact made with famous explorer). Some of the favorite stories of Cape hauntings follow.

BEECHWOOD INN, BARNSTABLE

The Beechwood Inn is said to be haunted by spirits of the departed. The inn's alleged resident ghost has been described as an old woman with long gray hair and dressed in a long white gown. Mark Jasper, author of *Haunted Inns of New England*, wrote, "When I was at the Beechwood, I was having breakfast. The tables there have these long white tablecloths, and I saw the corner of one begin to flutter like someone was pulling on it. There was no wind. There was no reason that would have happened."

According to a website on spooky places (www.gothichorrorstories.com), the resident ghost was nicknamed the "Mischievous Lady" by innkeepers Ken and Debra Traugot. A *Boston Globe* story reported that investigators of paranormal phenomena have been to the inn, and the owners say their ghost is responsible for "mysteriously unscrewing light bulbs, bolting doors shut from the inside and other, well, mischief."

One strange incident, described in a *Barnstable Patriot* article, involved a young couple who visited the inn with their baby. The couple woke up to find their baby lying between them, even though the baby had been put to sleep in a crib at the foot of the bed. Their daughter was too young to have crawled into bed with them. The reported ghost has also visited the owners, sometimes appearing in different rooms. Debra said she heard a woman's voice say "good morning" even though no one was with her. The CAIPRS report asserted that the inn has witnessed moving objects and voices. The ghost seems friendly and perhaps still feels a sense of propriety in taking care of the property and its inhabitants.

THE ORLEANS INN

The Orleans Inn, also known as the Orleans Waterfront Inn, has long been a known hot spot for ghosts. The *Cape Cod Guide* noted that two ghosts were believed to occupy the 125-year-old former mansion built by Captain Aaron Snow in 1875. One woman was believed to have thrown herself from the cupola that tops the building. Various manifestations of ghosts include "mysterious happenings such as lights going on, doors opening and closing or faucets turning on in unoccupied rooms." The CAIPRS report lists the inn as featuring moving objects, footsteps, fires relit and ghostly voices.

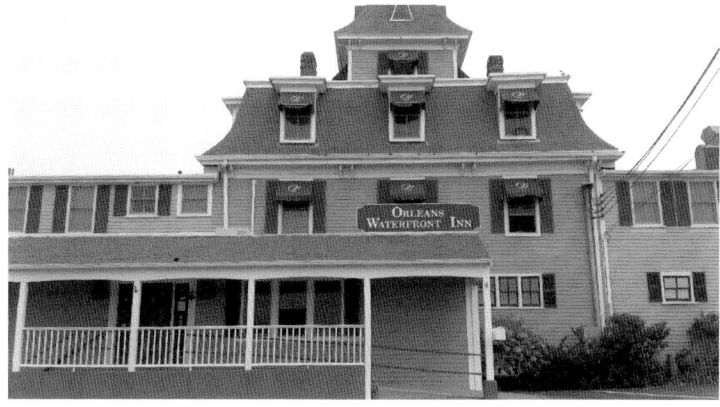

The Orleans Waterfront Inn. *Courtesy of Cynthia Sherrick Mitchell.*

A favorite family story has been retold by my mother many times. When my parents proposed a move to Cape Cod in 1961, they took an exploratory trip to make sure they were making the right decision. Arriving during a winter snowstorm, they opted to stay at the Orleans Inn. Since neither of my parents had ever visited Cape Cod before, they had no idea what they were walking into. The weather must have scared off other potential visitors because my parents were the only ones staying at the inn the night they arrived. They expected a quiet night but instead were kept awake by footsteps, slamming doors and, of course, the howling wind outside. Thankfully, the ghosts didn't deter my parents, and we moved to Rock Harbor Road in Orleans that June.

THE LEGEND OF MARY DUNN

In a tucked-away corner of Cape Cod sits Mary Dunn Pond. An old Indian woman lived here two hundred years ago. Mary Dunn was known as a fortune-teller and a prophet. She lived away from the world, preferring her own company. She studied the stars and collected herbs. Although the curious sought her out, she didn't seek human companionship. It was said she came ashore from a Swedish vessel wrecked on Sandy Neck during a fierce storm. Townspeople feared her because they thought she was the reason for the shipwreck that brought her to their shores. A large contingent of men hunted her down, but she was so calm and unresisting that she was let go. Her response to them was, "All is mystery and shall forever remain so. I am the last of a great and noble race."

She built herself a thatch hut and lived there for many years. Her age was indeterminate, but it seemed she was always ancient. According to an article written by Charles Warner Swift in 1896, "Her shrill, peculiar whistle, which resounded from the overhanging shades of the dense growth, brought from its fastnesses the timid deer, from its borough the fox, from its hole the rabbit, from the swamp the snake." Once she was reportedly found in a stupor with a large adder around her neck and one on each ankle. The woodsman who discovered her rushed to town to announce her ghastly death. Before he returned, she had roused herself, feeling ill from the intoxicating effects of one of her herbal potions.

Little is known of her life, but like another local legend, the witch Liza Tower Hill, Mary Dunn speaks to another time, when wisdom was gained from communing with nature and healing practiced with herbs and wise counsel.

A HAUNTED LIBRARY

There are many private dwellings with a haunted past, but legend has it that Cape Cod has a haunted library. Hyannis Public Library is said to be home to several ghosts, according to members of the Massachusetts Paranormal Institute. They have done research at the library as recently as 2009 and 2014. The most telling results came from EMF readings. An EMF meter can detect fluctuations in electromagnetic fields, and this is thought to reveal paranormal activity. Recordings are made that, when played back, sometimes appear to reveal ghostly voices.

The library was officially established in 1865, and its first full-time librarian, Ora Adams Hinckley, a former schoolteacher, served from 1909 until her death in 1943. She is believed to be one of the ghosts that resides in the library's stacks. There is even a wing named after her—the Ora Hinckley wing, the oldest part of the library. In the 2009 investigation, researchers asked Ora direct questions and received a soft "no" when asked if she got along with a former colleague. Staff members have said they sometimes smell pipe smoke, which might indicate a former employee, George Kelly, who liked to smoke his pipe in the building, is in the vicinity. Perhaps the most enigmatic ghost contact was that of a small child. He said his name was Nathan, and when asked if he would like to be left

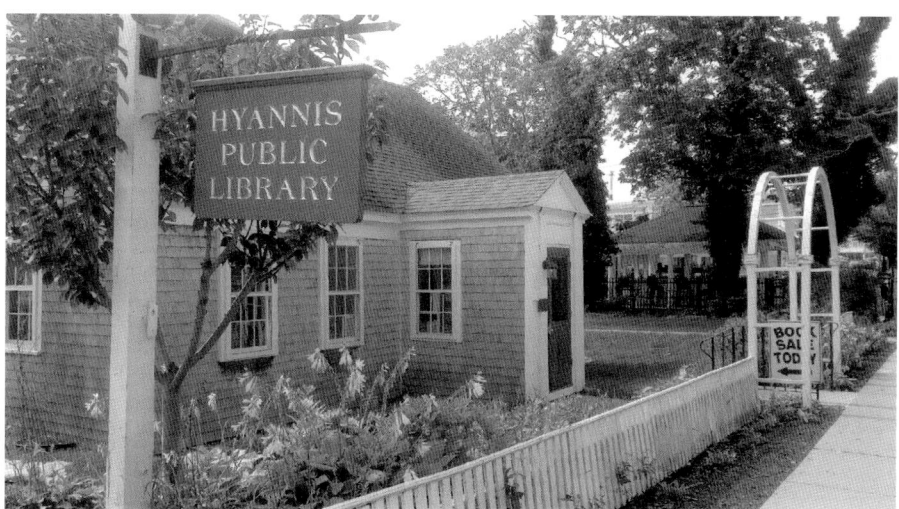

A front view of the Hyannis Public Library. *Courtesy of Gregory R. Johnson.*

alone, he answered "that would be nice." Several other strange events have happened, including a stack of books falling and a librarian who found the image of a book on ghosts on her computer screen that had not been there before. This was in 2014, when renovations were being done to the library, and it was thought that the ghosts disliked the activity and disruption going on. The Ora Hinckley wing has been designated a Certified Haunted Location, and every Halloween, the library hosts an expert in ghostly research to speak at the library.

A PERSONAL GHOST STORY

When I was ten years old, my family moved from Rock Harbor Road to Main Street in East Orleans. The house we moved into was large and old (dating back to the mid-nineteenth century). At night, the pipes creaked and moaned, scaring my sisters and me as we slept in adjoining bedrooms. Sometimes I woke up suddenly out of a deep sleep and thought someone was sitting on the end of my bed. If there was a ghost, however, it felt more friendly than menacing.

Connected to the main house by a breezeway was the barn that housed my parents' antiques and book shop, the Incredible Barn. On the wood planks of the second floor, deep in the dark shadows of the loft overlooking the shop, were dark stains. My father told us they were bloodstains from corpses piled there after the *Portland* steamer went down in the huge gale of 1898. Apparently, wreckage and bodies were washed ashore all along the backside of Cape Cod. The legend was that our house had been owned by the town undertaker and that some of the bodies discovered were stored in the barn before burial. Regardless of whether there was any truth to this historical legend, it impressed our young minds. I would spend my Saturdays going through boxes of my dad's books on that second-floor landing, but when nighttime approached, I always left well before the sun set.

My parents told us about the couple who sold them the house. It seems they often heard footsteps and noises coming from various parts of the drafty house. There was, in particular, a door that separated the kitchen pantry from the dining room. It was set on hinges that made the door hard to open, yet they claimed this door would swing back and forth when the owner sat to read at night. She tried, time after time, to wedge it shut, but the door always creaked open. Later, the house sat vacant for a year before our large family moved in. To help us open the house, my grandparents came for what was supposed to be a week's visit. They stayed only one night. My grandfather later explained that it was just too noisy.

We lived in the East Orleans house for ten years. Perhaps the resident ghosts became used to us because we didn't experience anything too scary until the last few months before we moved out. They may have sensed we were leaving and weren't happy. One day, my mother swore that she saw a face at the kitchen window. It wasn't anyone she knew and seemed to be hovering in midair. On another day, our family was settled in the living room when all the windows closed simultaneously. We jumped and stared around. There was no explanation for it. One morning shortly before we moved out of our beloved house, I was looking out the kitchen window and a row of bikes fell over, all at the exact same moment.

In a 2004 *Cape Cod Times* article, contributing writer Gary Joseph (co-author of *Cape Encounters*) wrote about his childhood. "As a Hyannis native, I grew up in a house where mysterious footsteps and loud crashes were often heard coming from empty upstairs rooms." He went on to wonder if ghost tales are true and why they seem to be prevalent on Cape Cod. "I've heard that ghosts like damp places with lots of atmosphere." I guess the Cape fits the bill.

CAPE COD VISIONARIES

MARCONI'S VISION

Cape Cod is host to a number of historic places, but perhaps none is as unique as the Marconi Station in South Wellfleet. Finished in 1902, the Marconi Station was the first U.S. transatlantic wireless telegraph station, which transmitted the first-ever wireless telegram on January 19, 1903.

Guglielmo Marconi was born in Bologna, Italy, in April 1874. The second son of Giuseppe Marconi and Annie Jamison, he was privately educated and, as a young boy, was especially interested in physical and electrical science. In 1895, he began conducting experiments with wireless radio signaling at his father's home in Pontecchio. In 1896, he traveled to England and was granted a patent for a system of wireless telegraphy. He was able to demonstrate the system's ability to transmit radio signals. Wireless telegraphy is communication via electrical signals but without electrical wires to connect the end points. A *Cape Cod Times* article reported that "[Marconi] quickly eclipsed all records for transmission distance with 8.7 miles in 1897, 34 miles in 1900 and over 50 miles from ship to ship in 1899."

He built one station in Poldhu, England, with two, 150-foot ship masts serving as antennas. His first successful transatlantic transmission was sent from Poldhu to St. John's, Newfoundland, 1,700 miles away. He used the Morse code letter "S." Shortly after, he moved to Wellfleet and built four 210-foot towers in the bluffs. It was the perfect place for him to transmit

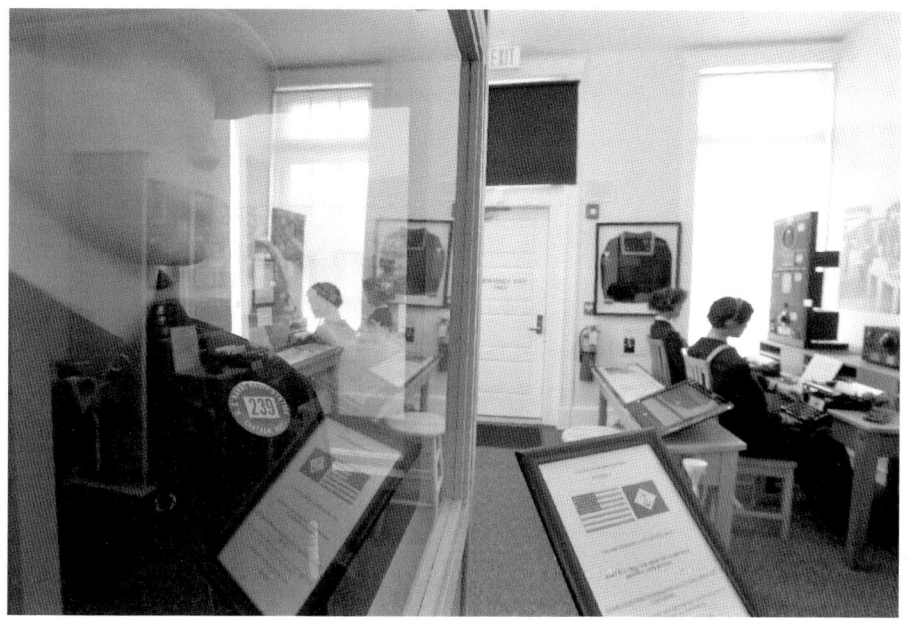

A mock-up of a pair of navy radio operators from the days of the Chatham Navy Radio Station. *Courtesy of the* Cape Cod Times.

messages. On January 18, 1903, his first actual transmission took just four minutes and contained greetings from President Theodore Roosevelt. The return transmission from England held a message from King Edward. Later, the Wellfleet station was abandoned and the towers destroyed in 1920.

According to Erik Barnouw in his book *A History of Broadcasting*, Marconi's obsession was not voice, but distance. This fact would become haunting reality in 1912 when the station detected the first telegraphed distress message from the doomed *Titanic*.

But this wasn't the end of Marconi's vision. In 1914, he built a large campus overlooking Ryder's Cove in Chatham. Here, he constructed fifteen buildings on the 104-acre site to be a part of a global wireless communication network. Later, the Radio Corporation of America bought the site in 1920 and eventually sold it to MCI. Guglielmo Marconi died in Rome on July 20, 1937, at age sixty-three.

In January 2003, Guglielmo Marconi's daughter, Princess Elettra Marconi, helped to commemorate one hundred years of wireless technology. She relayed a message to the International Space Station. Her message was, "One-hundred years ago today, my father Guglielmo Marconi sent the first wireless message across the Atlantic Ocean from Cape Cod. In this same spirit of his achievement and also from Cape Cod, I send this wireless message: 'Cordial greetings, good wishes and God bless you.'"

Like father, like daughter. The twin spirits navigated great distances and made Cape history.

CHARLES AYLING: THE FOUNDING OF CAPE COD HOSPITAL

On October 3, 1920, an article in the *Boston Daily Globe* proudly announced, "Hospital for All Cape Cod Opens Tomorrow at Hyannis." Before the building of a local hospital, injured fishermen and women facing difficult pregnancies had to travel by train to Boston hospitals. There was also the fear that a return of the influenza epidemic might strike. In part due to these concerns, the Visiting Nurse Association of Cape Cod was formed in 1916 so that nurses would be available for people needing medical help.

Charles Ayling, a local businessman, was instrumental in envisioning the need for a Cape hospital. In 1918, as he was riding in a train, he witnessed two Belgian sailors being taken to Boston for treatment after they were shipwrecked off Cape Cod shores in stormy seas. For two days, they were frozen to the mast of their ship. In his book *The Last Five Decades: Cape Cod Hospital*, Larry G. Newman wrote, "There was only one way to rescue them—cut them away, bandage them hastily and get them on the train to Boston, where they could receive medical treatment." Ayling saw clearly that Cape Cod needed its own hospital. Later, Ayling donated the money needed to build a new wing that still bears his name. He also served as president of the hospital's corporation for eleven years until he stepped down in 1942.

Another fascinating fact about Charles Ayling is that he was the first person to drive a car on Cape Cod. In 1902, he drove his Stanley Steamer from Centerville to Provincetown over sand roads. People were so afraid his car might explode that he was asked to park it overnight in a field. That first automobile trip took an entire day to complete. Thankfully, it only takes ninety minutes now to drive his original route.

Looking back to that long-ago *Globe* announcement, the words almost fly off the page. "Cape Cod now has a hospital for its exclusive use. The new Cape Cod Hospital is located on what was the old Watts estate, adjoining that of Dr. Gleason's, bordering on the Park and Bayview area. It will open tomorrow, Monday, available for patients from all points of the Cape." There is also a photo of Miss Nellie E. Woodworth, the new superintendent. The article stated that she was a Boston woman and graduate of the New England Hospital. Her straightforward gaze seems to promise confidence and efficiency at the start of a new endeavor.

We take for granted our easy access to medical care, but it was not always the case for Cape Codders. Thanks to Ayling, the Hyannis Board of Trade and many others, the Cape Cod Hospital (now part of Cape Cod Healthcare) thrives as it serves the Cape population.

A Plimoth Plantation Original: Henry Hornblower II

The Plimoth Plantation was the brainchild of Boston stockbroker Henry Hornblower II. Born in 1917, Hornblower spent his childhood summers in Plymouth, and the idea for the plantation came to him very early in life. He spent many hours studying the town's history and exploring the lands around his summer home, the Hornblower estate. His early love for archaeology was fostered by the Hornblower gardener, Jessie Brewer. He fell in love with the Pilgrim story and wanted to find a way to bring it to life.

After graduating from Harvard with a degree in archaeology in 1941 and also serving his country during World War II, Henry persuaded his father to give the Pilgrim society $20,000 to purchase land and prepare plans for a re-created Pilgrim village. In his obituary (published on October 23, 1985, in the *Cape Cod* Times), Harry was quoted as saying, "Our goal was simple. We just wanted to tell the Pilgrim story." Harry went on to become a chartered financial analyst and a partner for many years in the Hornblower & Weeks, Hemphill-Noyes Firm.

In October 1947, Plimouth Plantation was established as a nonprofit corporation. It began with a "First House" exhibit, where the *Mayflower II* is presently docked, but quickly became an expanded village. According to the Plimoth Plantation website, "Plimoth Plantation, a bicultural museum, offers powerful personal encounters with history built on thorough research about the Wampanoag People and the Colonial English community in the 1600s." Costumed staff members play the roles of the original Pilgrims and crew, as well as members of

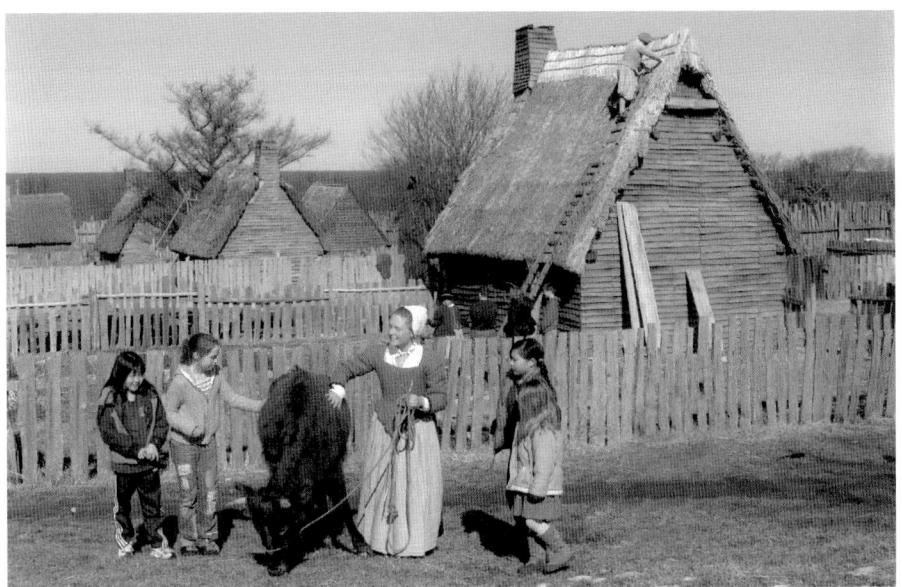

A costumed woman with a cow and curious children at the Plimoth Plantation. *Courtesy of the* Cape Cod Times.

the Wampanoag Nation. Incidentally, the Pilgrims were first identified by their descendants as the "forefathers," and the name "Pilgrim" didn't come into use until the American Revolution.

History buff and dreamer Henry Hornblower II died at age sixty-seven of a heart attack. His legacy and unique vision live on. Time at Plimoth Plantation is always set in the year 1627, and visitors from all over the world have come to learn its lore and treasures.

OLD SCHOOLHOUSES

A LINK TO THE PAST

There are many old one-room schoolhouses on Cape Cod, but one that has been preserved for future generations is the Cataumet Schoolhouse. Built off County Road in 1894, the schoolhouse was used by students for several decades until it was closed to students in 1930 and neglected for many years.

The building piqued the interest of the town, and in 1999, the Cataumet Schoolhouse Preservation Group convinced town officials to scrap plans to move the school across town and instead to restore it in the village where it had always stood. The schoolhouse was on the annual list of threatened landmarks published by Historic Massachusetts, a pictorial travel map. The Bourne selectmen listened to the town's citizens and voted to keep the schoolhouse in its original site in 2000. The following year, neighbors sued the group and the Town of Bourne to reverse a zoning board of appeals variance that allowed construction of a period-style outhouse complete with running water and modern toilets.

The preservation group searched for period items to use in the restoration. It hunted down southern yellow pine, used in the original doors; scoured the internet to find the same bell the town bought in the early 1920s; found an old photo of Abraham Lincoln to hang in the classroom; and replaced more than half of the building's windows. In August 2003, the schoolhouse acquired a new 1,400-pound belfry. Future goals include acquiring period desks for the school, restoring the chalkboards, building a playground that replicates the nineteenth-century playground and building a boys' and girls' outhouse.

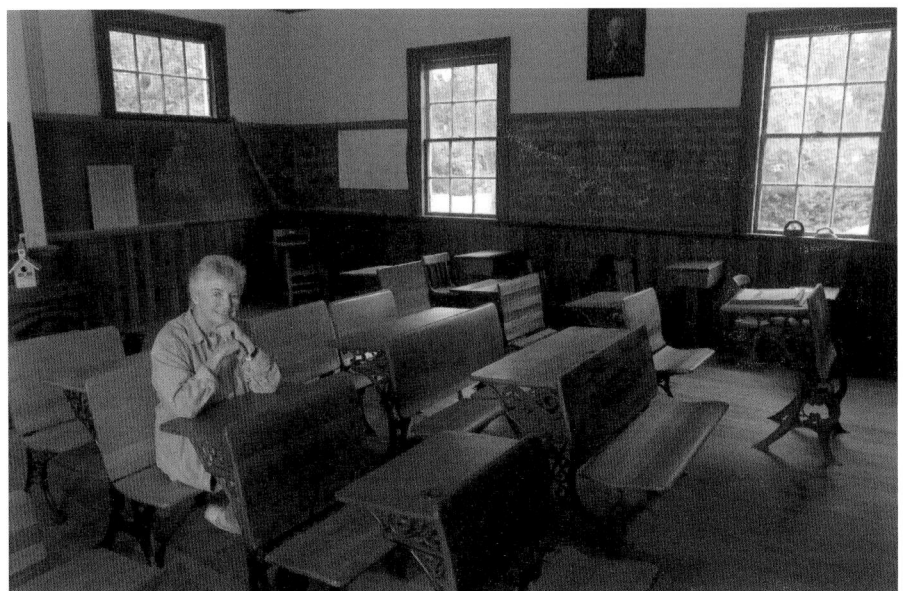

An interior shot of the Cataumet Schoolhouse, built in 1894. *Courtesy of the* Cape Cod Times.

Since the goal of the preservation group is to restore the school as an education facility, museum and community meeting place, it is a place that today's children and their parents can enjoy. The gray clapboard walls and black shutters are welcoming, as are the double doors (possibly originally used as separate entrances for girls and boys).

Another former one-room schoolhouse was located in Eastham and built in 1869. One of four similar one-room schoolhouses at the time, it housed Grades 1 through 8. In 1906 and 1907, two of the other three schoolhouses were moved to the site and combined. Its final year of operation was in 1936. Former students remembered the little school fondly. In a 2003 *Cape Cod Times* article, the memories described were both visual and olfactory. A 1933 graduate remembered the school's unique odor as "peanut butter sandwiches and corduroy pants." There was a big brown stove stoked twice a day and a stone crock filled with fresh drinking water. Ice from a nearby pond was used to make grape nut ice cream on Valentine's Day.

In these small towns, children learned by reciting and were helped with their studies by the older students. Their parents were farmers and shellfishermen. Those who had recently moved to town were called "Outsiders," another name for "Wash-a-Shores." Children traveled to school in a bus known as the "school barge," with its "canvas roll-up sides, and kids tying their sleds on the back of the bus so they could use them at recess." In 2008, the town of Eastham celebrated the grand opening of the schoolhouse and museum.

In Mashpee, home to the Wampanoag Indians, the town's one-room schoolhouse was built in 1831. It served as a school for fifteen families until 1901, when it was sold to the Young People's Baptist Society for twenty-two dollars. After changing hands many times, it was returned to the town in 1975. After extensive renovations, the schoolhouse was opened for visitors in May 2009. According to a *Cape Cod Times* article, the schoolhouse "is a time machine, complete with eight benches for 'students,' a pine replica teacher's desk, individual slates for each student, quills and inkwells and lanterns." The schoolhouse is a reminder of a native people from a bygone era who invested in their children and passed down their traditions.

The life of a schoolteacher in those early days was hard. The pay was mcagcr, and a young man or woman might get lonely living in an isolated Cape town. In her book *Earning a Living on Olde Cape Cod*, author Marion Vuilleumier described the typical one-room schoolhouse: "There were two rows of unpainted plank desks and backless seats about 10 feet long. Girls sat on one side and boys on the other. A fireplace and the teacher's pine boxlike desk were at the front." Towns did not provide necessary supplies, so students had to bring their own books, pens, ink and paper. Children also had to bring in firewood to help keep the schoolhouse warm. Discipline was another problem since the older boys had to take time off in the spring and summer to work on fishing vessels, so they only attended school in the winter. Fortunately, things began to improve over time. With the advent of World War II, one-room schoolhouses were phased out and replaced with bigger, more modern schools.

OLD-FASHIONED HOLIDAYS

Cape Codders have always enjoyed celebrating the holidays. The daily round of chores was enlivened by family traditions, from cutting down a pine tree to festoon with lights at Christmas to setting off fireworks and enjoying a clam bake on the Fourth of July. These stories relate the festivities, poems and merrymaking of holidays long ago.

Cape Cod has been home to many writers who have enriched our artistic landscape. One native author was country doctor Dr. Thomas Newcomb Stone (1818–1876). He made his home in the center of Wellfleet on a hill sometimes still referred to as "Dr. Stone's Hill."

Dr. Stone was a hardworking family doctor who only charged families two dollars to deliver a baby. He was also sought out for his wit and humor as a motivational speaker. In the parlance of the time, he was described as having a "strong physique, stately appearance, cliff-like brow and a keen eye for a sense of humor." The profession of doctor ran in his family, as his father (Dr. William Stone) and his son (Dr. William Newcomb Stone) were also physicians. Dr. Stone was a thirty-year member of the Wellfleet School Committee and was instrumental in having the Wellfleet High School and the Fishermen's School moved from the outskirts of town to its center so students would have a shorter walk to school.

However, it is as a poet, or rhyme maker, that Dr. Stone is remembered now. His poems were compiled in an 1869 book called *Cape Cod Rhymes*. On December 31, 1873, he had a Christmas carol published in the *Provincetown Advocate*:

Last night of mother mild
In stable born
Israel's hope and joy,
The Christ was born
And sages old and wise
In regions far,
Saw, mid the orbs of night
A new-lit star
This morn bright angels sang
To greet the day
Peace to the troubled earth
In sweetest lay,
Most wondrous child, earth-born,
My soul to Thee
With seers and sages old,
Would bow the knee.
My heart's sweet hope and joy,
My gracious Lord,
May this brief life of mine
With thine accord,
Then from its sky serene,
Each conflict still,
Shall come the angel song,
Peace and good will.

HOLIDAY COUNTDOWN, 1936

The *Cape Cod Standard Times* began life in 1936 as a subsidiary paper to the *New Bedford Standard Times*, not gaining its own status as the *Cape Cod Times* until 1974. In 1936, another Cape paper was started, the *Cape Cod Colonial*. This upstart only lasted one year. In the interest of a bias-free account of that first Christmas countdown, a look through articles in both papers offers a sense of what Cape Codders were doing in December 1936.

On December 11, 1936, the world was drawn to the news that Edward, King of England, was stepping down from the throne to marry the twice-divorced Mrs. Wallis Simpson. He had reigned for only 327 days. His brother, the Duke of York, George VI, was made king on December 12,

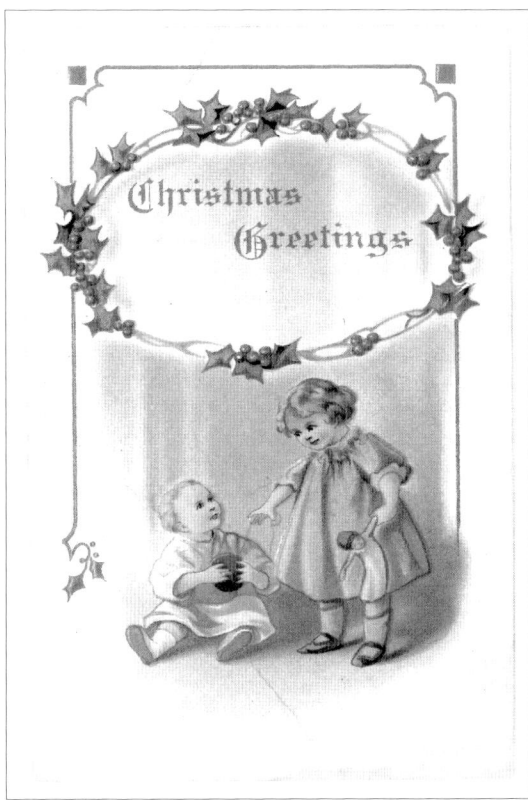

Left: A vintage Christmas card. *From the postcard collection of Wendell E. Smith.*

Below: An old "Rally Day" postcard inviting children to come to Sunday school. *From the postcard collection of Wendell E. Smith.*

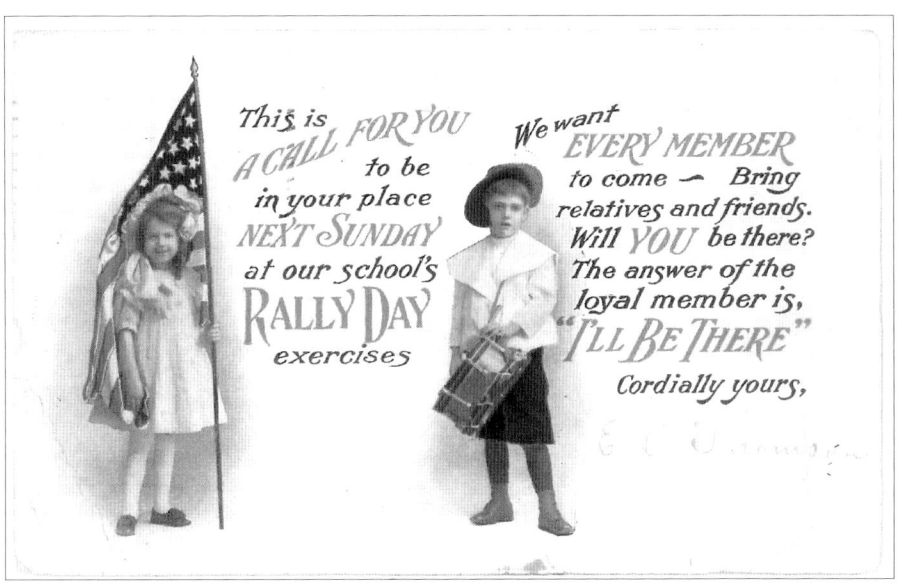

1936. His two daughters were Elizabeth and Margaret. In the same issue, an article titled "Home-Knit Mittens College Girls Favorite" showcased some ideas for homemade Christmas gifts.

On December 15, a blurb announced that the *Register* newspaper in Yarmouth was celebrating its 100th birthday. On December 21, Bass River was hit by a windstorm ("Home Suffers from Sudden Nor'easter"), and a cartoon showed a downtrodden mother and child looking into a toy store. The caption reads, "But honey, Santa can't get everywhere." This seems a stark reminder that Cape Codders were in the midst of the Great Depression. Also on this day, a Noel pageant was performed at Pilgrim Church in Harwich. A photo shows the expectant faces of children in the front row, as well as older girls behind them with banners that read "Sacrifice," "Service," "Peace" and "Worship." There was also an installment of Henry Beston's *The Outermost House*.

On December 22, the day's headline read, "Six Saved; Coast Guard Plane Lands in 15-ft. Seas." The article alerted readers to the forty-mile-per-hour gales battering Provincetown. In the same edition, a fashion shoot had the lead, "Tailored Chic for Miami Nights" and included a sampling of dessert recipes, including steamed carrot pudding, Pennsylvania plum pudding and holiday fruit cake. On December 23, the R.R. Higgins Oyster Company of Wellfleet announced that its doors were closing after 108 years in business. December 24 turned up a short story by Joseph Lincoln called "A Christmas Memory."

On December 26, an article noted that "better conditions make Christmas a great day and a big day for travel." A month-in-review cartoon wrapped up the big local stories:

- Cotuit has a new water system.
- *Atlantis* sails for gulf waters from Woods Hole.
- Sea Plane down off Provincetown.
- A wind storm in Bass River.
- Christmas lights cover the Cape.
- No more oysters at Wellfleet (Higgins & Co. closed).

Finally, there was a cartoon showing Santa in bed with his beard sticking out over the blankets. The caption read, "Tuckered out and tucked in."

HAPPY BIRTHDAY TO THE GRAND OLD FLAG

On June 14, 1777, the Continental Congress in Philadelphia adopted the Stars and Stripes as the national flag. This special day is now celebrated as Flag Day. The origin for a special day commemorating the flag dates back to 1885, when a schoolteacher, Bernard J. Cigrand, had his students in Wisconsin observe a "flag birthday." Many other schools adopted the idea, and in 1894, the mayor of New York directed that on June 14 the flag should be displayed on all public buildings. Finally, Flag Day was officially established by President Woodrow Wilson on May 30, 1916, but it wasn't until August 3, 1949, that President Harry Truman signed an act of Congress designating June 14 as National Flag Day.

One place that has taken Flag Day to heart is the Forestdale School in Sandwich. The elementary school has held Flag Day ceremonies since 1990, organized by teacher Carol Quill. On June 14, 1996, more than nine hundred students watched Coast Guard and U.S. Army helicopters land on the back field of the school. Students then got into the spirit of the day by reciting historical texts and singing patriotic songs. Mashpee also got into the act in 1996 with a festive town parade that proceeded along Steeple Street into the Mashpee Commons.

In 1998, Sarah Lindblad, age nine, donated a flag that had belonged to her grandfather Patrick Lauzier. He was a navy and air force veteran of World War II and the Korean War. Students at the Forestdale School also painted flags on their faces and waved small flags as the festivities unfolded. On June 14, 2002, students unveiled a 104- by 84-foot American flag quilt, created from patches brought in by schoolchildren. Those in attendance remembered U.S. Navy captain Gerald DeConto, a Sandwich native, who died on September 11, 2001, during the terrorist attack on the Pentagon. On June 15, 2005, the *Cape Cod Times* ran a photo montage of places all over Cape Cod showing their Stars and Stripes, including Harwich, Yarmouth Port, Hyannis, Wareham and Dennis. People interviewed mentioned the flag in many different ways: freedom, sacrifice, honor, bravery and more.

Flag Day is often a day people retire their old flags. In fact, the United States flag code reads, "The flag represents a living country and is itself considered a living thing."

SQUEAK THE FIFE: CELEBRATING INDEPENDENCE DAY

How was the Fourth of July celebrated in the early days of Cape Cod? Massachusetts was the first state to officially recognize the holiday in 1781. In the early days, Cape towns rang church bells, held parades with drum and bugle corps and brought out ancient fire engines and Model A Fords. The Fourth of July also served as a Field Day, where kids would take part in paddle and hoop races, lawn bowling, potato spoon races and a corn bag toss.

Parades have always been a staple for each Cape town. From Chatham to Cotuit, Wellfleet to Woods Hole, each village and town puts its own stamp on the holiday. Various clubs and neighborhoods would have cannon firings and block parties. There were also bonfires, sailboat races and boat parades (often called "floating" parades).

In the 1960s and '70s, the Cape was inundated with tourists, and Fourth of July weekend was often marred by rowdy parties and car accidents. Debris from fireworks sometimes caused brush fires. In 1976, the Cape celebrated the nation's bicentennial with festivities that included the return of the Tall Ships (a large, traditionally rigged sailing vessel). Today, the traditions of parades and fireworks are as popular as ever. A poem that appeared in the *Farmer's Weekly Museum* in 1800 read, "Squeak the fife and beat the drum/Independence Day is come!/Come foot it, Sal: Moll, figure in/And, mother, you dance up to him/Thus we dance and thus we play,/On glorious Independence Day!"

TALES OF THE LOWER CAPE

Eastham Only Cape Town Founded by Pilgrims

A little-known fact is that Eastham was the only town on Cape Cod founded by Pilgrims. It was originally home to the Nauset Indians.

In 1643, a group of Pilgrims, dissatisfied with the barren soil and small allotment of land given to them, set out to find a new home. The Plymouth church sent out a committee to examine the Nauset Indian Territory. Seven of the group decided to stay: Edward Bangs, Josias Cook, John Doane, Richard Higgins, Thomas Prence, John Smalley and Nicholas Snow. They were impressed by the rich soil and abundant forests of the area. Today, about 11 percent of Eastham is part of the Cape Cod National Seashore.

In 1644, these "old comers" (who arrived either on the *Mayflower*, the *Fortune* or the *Ann*) brought their families to Nauset, forty-nine people in all. Two years later, the town was incorporated, and the name was changed to Eastham in 1651. The name may have come from the town of Eastham in Cheshire, John Doane's former home, or from East Ham, a suburb of London in Essex County.

Eastham's first board of selectmen was appointed in 1663: John Freeman, Nicholas Snow and John Doane. True to its Puritan traditions, the town set up a public whipping post and stocks in 1695. Later, two areas of Eastham seceded to become Wellfleet in 1763 and Orleans in 1797. Farming was one of the main occupations of the town, with cranberries and asparagus as two of the major crops. Fisheries flourished, with both cod and oysters shipped north. In the late nineteenth century, the town went into an economic decline that ended only after World War II, when tourism helped to give the town new direction.

350TH ANNIVERSARY OF THE PILGRIM LANDING

In 1970, the town of Provincetown had a celebration on the anniversary of the Pilgrims' landing. On November 21, 1970, Provincetown selectmen and the 350th Committee planted a symbolic cedar tree, and some forty men, including selectmen, reenacted the signing of the Mayflower Compact in Plymouth. Henry Lehne, assistant postmaster, delivered an address at the dedication of a six-cent postage stamp commemorating the landing of the Pilgrims at Plymouth. Because the Pilgrims landed first at Provincetown before settling in Plymouth, the ceremony took place in both Plymouth and Provincetown.

On November 20, 1970, Provincetown children took part in "Reenactment Day." Sixth-graders presented their interpretation of the first Pilgrim wash day. When the Pilgrims came ashore that historic day, the first thing they did was to wash their clothes. After their presentation, the students traveled by bus to Truro, where a group of fifth-grade students presented a pageant in memory of Corn Hill, the place where the men found corn to bring back to the ship. The group then traveled to Wellfleet to view a program about the cutting of a blackfish by the Indians, and the day ended in Eastham, where students and staff reenacted the first skirmish between the Pilgrims and the Indians at First Encounter Beach.

Another way the town celebrated the Pilgrims' landing was the lighting of Pilgrim Monument in early October. The lights were then lit each night throughout the rest of the year. In honor of the anniversary, President Richard Nixon sent congratulations to the town. His message read in part: "Three hundred and fifty years ago, Massachusetts cradled the intrepid spirit of liberty and justice that has become the life-giving symbol of our national experience. Throughout those years, our citizens have drawn strength, encouragement and hope from the celebrated achievement of our Pilgrim fathers.…I join with you in recalling an event that continues to be a revitalizing force in the lives of all of us." He also sent a letter to Governor Francis Sargent to thank him for providing commemorative medals to mark the anniversary.

The lord mayor of Plymouth, England, paid a brief visit in October 1970 and placed a wreath at the foot of the Pilgrim Monument. A small contingent sailed to Plymouth on the Swedish-American liner *Kungsholm*. Unfortunately, the Provincetown town crier, eighty-five-year-old Fred Baldwin, fell ill on the boat ride and had to be taken to Jordan Hospital. When the party returned to Provincetown, officials fired a 340-year-old bronze cannon. In recognition of the event, the 400th anniversary of the Pilgrim landing will occur in 2020.

WELLFLEET'S PIECE OF THE ROCK

In April 1984, a front section of a rock that may have been the original marker between Wellfleet and Eastham was presented to outgoing Wellfleet selectman Warren Rhodes. A local collector of antiquities, Michael Parlante, had discovered the long-missing rock in the woods east of Route 6. He said that some old-timers had told him where it was. It had taken Parlante a week of digging to find the rock under the surface of the ground two years before. According to local historians, one of the first things the newly incorporated town did in 1763 was to set the marker between Wellfleet and Eastham.

In an old photo, selectman Rhodes is seen holding one side of the stone marker while a bearded Parlante holds it from the top. A large printed *W* is visible, along with a dividing line and the letter *E*. Weighing in at seventy pounds, this was no small stone. In a *Cape Cod Times* article published at the time of the presentation, Parlante explained that the rock was actually the front slice of a larger piece that split. It should be noted that Parlante had a long love for archaeology and kept the rock in his room before deciding to give it to the town. In later years, Parlante himself became a selectman, as well as a shellfisherman, aquaculturist and part owner of a popular Wellfleet restaurant.

In its early days, the town was called Poole, after Dorsetshire in England. However, the townspeople liked the name Wellfleet ("whale fleet") because it seemed more connected to the lives of these seafaring folks. The town later had nicknames like "Dogtown" and "Skunks Misery" because its famous supply of oysters diminished around 1870. Whatever their early origins, the people of Eastham and Wellfleet manage to get along, even without the comfort of a dividing line—or, in this case, stone.

CAPE COD TRADITIONS

Old-Fashioned Gardens: Easy to Create

On Cape Cod, as well as the rest of New England, gardens were meant to put food on the table. By contrast, many European gardens were created for their beauty and often laid out in formal patterns. As well as vegetables, the pioneer New England gardener planted herbs for flavor and medicines. Flowers were added sparingly for color and as a welcome to spring and summer.

The housewife was considered the expert of the house garden. She depended on her garden for all domestic needs, including dyeing, insect repellants, deodorants, plasters and salves and even for embalming. Walkways were mostly made of shells or gravel and needed to be wide enough for two people.

There was no formal garden plan; gardens were mostly designed for use and geography. Often they were divided between annuals and perennials but in no particular order. As a *Cape Cod Times* article recorded, "The most commonly used herbs would be planted closest to the kitchen or keeping room door, where the housewife could quickly pick a handful for flavoring stew or mixing a medicinal broth." The vegetable garden might be planted along a southern slope so that early vegetables could catch the warmest rays of the spring sun.

Parlor gardens consisted of flowers planted along the front walks of a house or a dooryard. These gardens were fenced and placed so guests sitting in the parlor could see them.

Nowadays, gardeners borrow ideas from the early settlers, including growing herbs for seasonings and garnishes. During the Cape Cod revival period in architecture from 1930 to 1955, homeowners would grow cottage gardens with a mix of new and traditional plants, with their plantings bordered with pebbles or shells.

CAPE COD STYLE HOUSES

The Cape Cod–style house began appearing in New England in the late seventeenth century. It is believed that Reverend Timothy Dwight, president of Yale University from 1752 to 1817 and who traveled around New England around 1800, came up with the name. Henry David Thoreau was a fan of this style as well. The term pertains to any one-story house with a gabled roof and central chimney. It was compact and inexpensive, and local materials were used in the construction. The style was most likely brought over from England by early settlers.

In order to keep the weather out and create attic space, the roofs were high pitched. To serve multiple fireplaces, a large center chimney was needed for heating and cooking. Wooden shingles covered roofs and walls, although clapboard was often used in inland houses. Shutters were also used. These houses were less expensive to build than a full two-story house.

There were three basic front elevations: half Cape, three-quarter Cape and full Cape. Each type of house could be easily expanded, especially if a growing family needed more space. An ell at the back of the house was the most common type of addition. A full Cape was sometimes called a double house and often had five bays. This two-and-a-half-story home had a center entry, with pairs of windows on each side. There were two front rooms and a long room running across the back level on the first floor. The second floor often featured a "captain's stairway," which was a narrow set of stairs used by children or boarders.

In more recent years, Boston architect Royal Barry Wills reintroduced the Cape Cod–style house in the 1920s, and the style gained prominence during the Colonial Revival trend in architecture from the 1930s to 1950s. Traditional Capes continue to be popular and are an important part of the Cape Cod landscape.

TROTTING HORSES AND SULKY RACING

It's hard to believe, but horse racing used to be a popular sport on Cape Cod. In her book *Harwich*, author Joan M. Maloney wrote that "good horses were always prized. A racetrack used to circle what is now Wychmere Harbor [in Harwich Port], and sulky races were well attended and hotly contested." Before the state dredged a proper channel for the harbor and there was direct access to the sea, a three-quarter-mile racetrack was built around Salt Water Pond for horse racing.

This early love for racing horses is evidenced by the many Cape Cod towns, from Falmouth to Yarmouth to West Dennis, that have at least one Trotting Park Road. In *The Names of Cape Cod*, Trotting Park Road is mentioned as being named for "a racetrack off the road in West Dennis, popular in town during the late 1800s." Trotting horses and sulky racing were also a highlight of the Barnstable County Fair years ago.

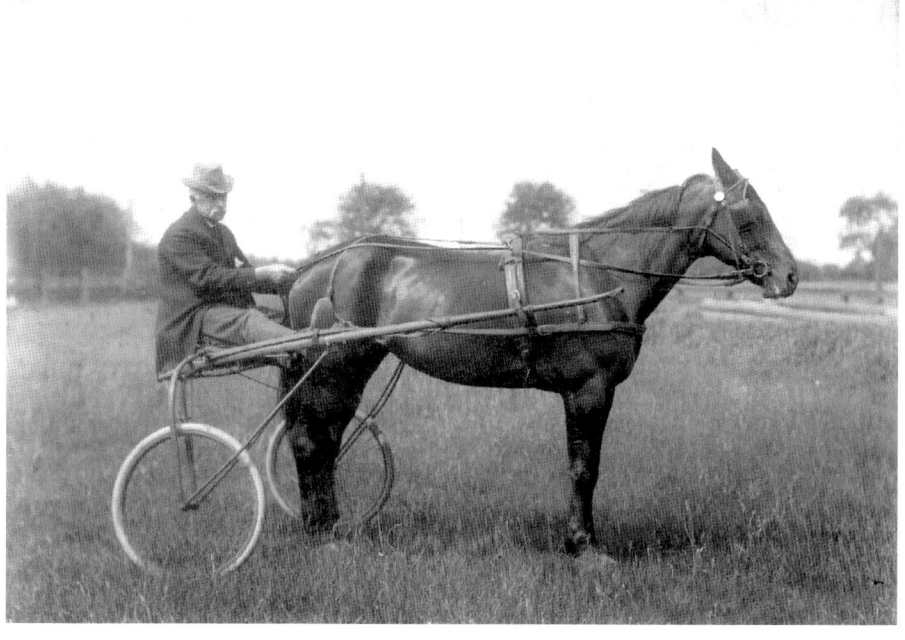

An antique photo of John Smith and his trotter. *Courtesy of the W.B. Nickerson Archives, Cape Cod Community College.*

ICE CREAM: A CAPE COD FAVORITE

One of the pleasures of a Cape Cod summer is rediscovering ice cream. From the Polar Cave in Mashpee to Four Seas Ice Cream in Centerville, there are many places to stop by and dip into a cone or cup. But did you know that ice cream made its Cape debut in 1902 when David Henry Sears of Dennis began making and selling the icy treat in his grocery store?

According to a 1976 *Cape Cod Times* excerpt, he made ice cream one gallon at a time. Since the modern freezer and refrigerator hadn't been invented yet, the refrigeration used was ice and salt packed tightly in a container from which water was drained frequently. Luckily, there was plenty of salt on Cape Cod, so this method was convenient for inventive Cape Codders. Sears was able to utilize his own dairy cows, his icehouse supplied the ice and his family helped out with the busy operation.

Gertrude Hodsdon of Dennis, Sears's granddaughter, had fond memories of growing up: "Tasting ice cream just after it was cranked was something which is just beyond comparison. We used all fresh fruits—and lots of it… through experimentation, we even came up with a 'fruit flavored ice cream' using fresh pineapple, banana and lemon." Of course, nowadays, there are countless flavors to choose from. We can also choose between soft-serve and hard ice cream, frappes and floats, sundaes and ice cream sandwiches.

Dick Warren, the original owner, who ran and operated Four Seas, said, "It's a fun business because you are dealing with a happy thing. Most people come in with smiles on their faces, anticipating what they are going to have." Sadly, the "ice cream man" died in January 2008, but his delicious message lives on.

HANDMADE SAMPLERS

In a time before cellphones and computers, young girls of the nineteenth century spent their spare time working on their sewing skills. They made samplers to show off their talent as budding seamstresses. A well-made sampler might also help a young woman attract a husband. In a 1984 *Cape Cod Times* article, Henry Callan, an expert on antique samplers, asserted that they were "an integral part of the education of school girls…and stood as an important symbol of their refinement." The samplers also told stories of the girls' lives, retelling events from home, school and family. A girl might also stitch a favorite verse and finish off her creation by including her name and the date of completion. The most valuable samplers for the collector and historian include this information.

Older women also created samplers as a sort of family register. A married woman might record births, deaths and marriages. The samplers also showed the maker's personality. Callan pointed to one that read, "Patty Polk did this and hated every stitch she did in it. She loves to read much more." Samplers were also a way to try different stitches and practice new techniques. The samplers might feature borders of flowers, household items or the alphabet.

When a young girl was finished with her sampler, instead of hanging it on a wall, she rolled it up and placed it in her sewing basket. These might have been part of a girl's eventual hope chest, those things she would bring with her when she married, later passing them down to her children.

POSTCARDS: A PEEK INTO THE PAST

One way to capture the bygone history of Cape Cod is by seeking out antique postcards. It is still possible to collect old postcards and capture a bit of the past. Barnstable's Sturgis Library has its own Cape Cod postcard collection, described in the Sturgis archives as a "collection of postcards with views of Cape Cod towns and villages from the collection of David Crocker of Mashpee, Massachusetts and Eldon Davidson, as well as other sources. Also includes views of the Cape Cod Canal, the cranberry industry, whales, ships, and lighthouses. Postcards date from approximately 1900 through the

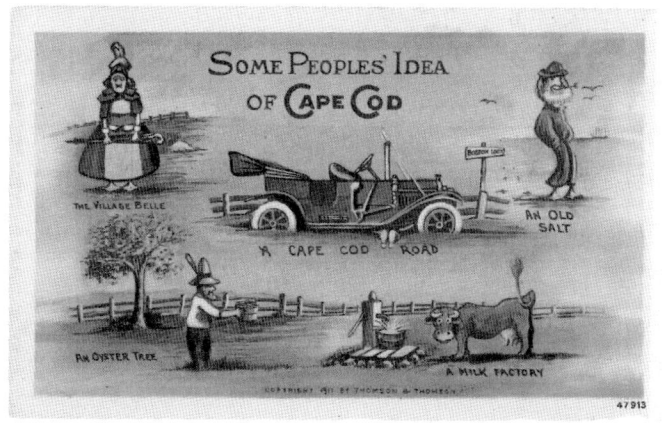

A whimsical postcard showing "Some Peoples' Idea of Cape Cod." *From the postcard collection of Wendell E. Smith.*

1970s." Sturgis Library is the oldest building that houses a public library in the United States.

One curious postcard that recently came to light shows a host of funny figures under the header "Some Peoples' Idea of Cape Cod." An old-fashioned automobile graces a "Cape Cod Road" with a sign pointing toward Boston. There is a white-bearded sea captain with a pipe clenched between his teeth, "An Old Salt." A stout lady with a stern expression and holding a cane is "The Village Belle." She is flanked by a farmer next to his "Oyster Tree" and holding out a canister to his "Milk Factory" (a surprised-looking cow). The humor is simple and reflects a bygone era.

The avid collector can find old Cape postcards at antique shops and antique sales. The Cape Cod Antique Dealers Association always hosts yearly events with multiple dealers under one roof. One can even browse eBay to find that rare postcard.

CAPE CODDERS AT WAR

Cape Codders have always had an independent streak. When the Revolutionary War seemed imminent, local residents were torn in their loyalties. The younger men supported the Patriots and were prepared to fight for the cause. Older, more conservative men were Tories or Loyalists to the British. James Otis, a young lawyer from Barnstable and a famous Patriot, delivered a fiery address before the Superior Court of Massachusetts against the use of "Writs of Assistance" by British customs officers. By the time war broke out, most Cape Codders were on the side of the Patriots, and a substantial militia from the Cape joined the revolutionary forces.

One unsung local hero was Captain John Hedge of Dennis, who commanded a militia company during the Revolutionary War. He was ultimately taken as a prisoner of war by the British and held on a British prison ship in New York Harbor. After he died in 1782, he was dumped overboard, although the war had officially ended six months earlier. A *Cape Cod Times* article mentioned that "a gray slab-covered brick monument in Dennis' Union Cemetery along Route 6A marks the memory of Capt. Hedge." Another fascinating fact is that many African American soldiers fought in the Revolutionary War, including sixty from Barnstable County.

In her book *Yesterday's Cape Cod*, author Evelyn Lawson wrote, "In 1775, Provincetown Harbor was a rendezvous for British men-of-war. The waters around the Cape tip had been designated as neutral territory, and the British took full advantage of the situation. They confiscated supplies from the inhabitants and, when short-handed, forced the town men to serve on their ships. Some of these men ended up in English prisons." After the war, restorations to wharves had to be made, and the economy took a long time to recover.

The Battle of Rock Harbor

On December 19, 1814, the Battle of Rock Harbor occurred during the War of 1812. British soldiers sent in a squadron of warships from the HMS *Newcastle* to patrol the bay and blockade Boston Harbor. They were also keeping an eye on Orleans, as the town had refused to pay ransom for protection. According to a *Cape Cod Times* article at the time of the battle's 200th anniversary celebration in 2014, a band of American militiamen from Orleans and neighboring towns prevented British soldiers from the *Newcastle* from pillaging a pier, boats and salt works. When the British came ashore, citizens from Orleans, Brewster and Eastham began firing. One British soldier was killed. Although this was a minor skirmish at the end of an unpopular war, it's a source of local pride that residents protected the Orleans shore from invasion.

The Civil War

Cape Codders also answered the call to fight during the Civil War. Slavery was not unheard of in Massachusetts; at least five local families owned slaves. In the summer of 1862, President Abraham Lincoln called for 300,000 troops to serve in the Union army for three years. According to historian Stauffer Miller, as many as 2,000 Cape Codders went to war. The Fortieth Massachusetts Volunteer Infantry was formed in August 1862, and all seven villages of Barnstable were represented.

In a *Cape Cod Times* article, it was noted that "for the next three years the regiment served in a number of major battles and skirmished in the outskirts of Washington, D.C. They took part in a chase after General Robert E. Lee in Maryland, helped build a bridge across the Potomac and the regiment witnessed a harrowing execution of a Union soldier." The young soldiers had to contend with illness (particularly malaria),

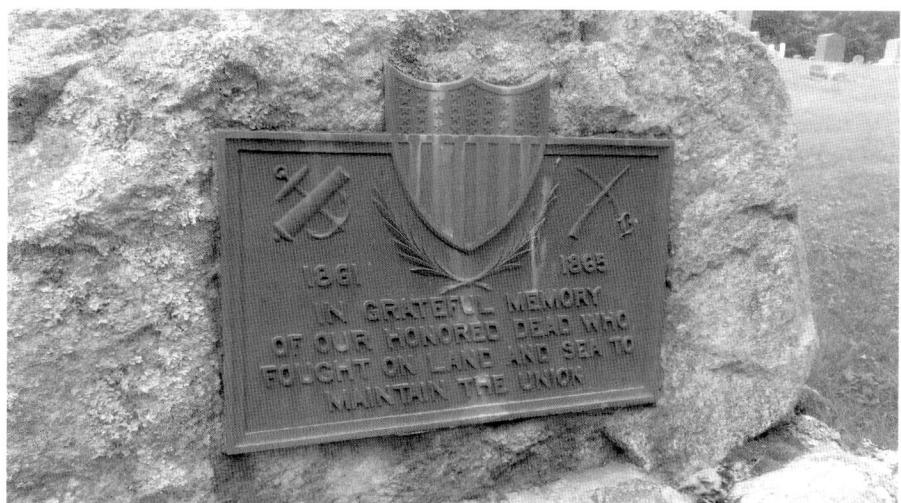

A granite stone Civil War memorial located in Beechwood Cemetery, Centerville. *Courtesy of Gregory R. Johnson.*

loneliness and homesickness. When the war ended, the soldiers returned to a weakened local economy, and many moved to other parts of the country to make their fortunes.

WORLD WAR I

When America decided to enter the war in 1917, many Cape Cod men signed up to serve. Little did they know they were headed to the horrific battlefield trenches of Europe, where mustard gas and gunfire would be turned against the Allied soldiers. According to veteran Laurence Moffitt of Orleans, as quoted in a *Cape Cod Times* article, "Such battle tactics were part of front-line living." When he was hit, the gas burned his skin, and he lost his voice. Many men came home with chronic respiratory illnesses as well as "shell shock," a condition we know today as PTSD or post-traumatic stress disorder. They also had to contend with the 1918 flu epidemic, which killed thousands. Some soldiers died from flu after the daily gas attacks weakened their lungs. More than 116,000 Americans lost their lives in what was known as the Great War, the "War to End All Wars."

PERTH AMBOY

Around 10:30 a.m. on July 21, 1918, a German submarine surfaced three miles off Orleans and fired on marshes and Nauset Beach. The *SM-U-156* of the imperial German army fired at the town and a passing tugboat, the *Perth Amboy*. The tugboat, along with four barges it was towing, was sunk. Nearby Station no. 40 of the United States Life-Saving Service launched a surfboat under heavy enemy shellfire and rowed out to rescue the thirty-two sailors trapped aboard the tug and barges. Fortunately, the crew was rescued, and although the captain was injured, there were no fatalities.

In his book *Orleans*, author Daniel Lombardo stated, "In September 1918, the only submarine to bomb United States soil in World War I struck a mine between Scotland and Norway and sank with its crew." Today, a sign above Nauset Beach commemorates the historic engagement: "Three miles offshore, in the direction of the arrow, was the scene of attack of a German submarine on a tug and barges July 21, 1918. Several shells struck the beach. This is the only section of the United States coast shelled by the enemy during World War I."

WORLD WAR II

After the Japanese bombed Pearl Harbor on December 7, 1941, a previously isolationist United States took up the call to arms. Cape Codders headed to Europe to join the Allied troops fighting the Nazi threat. Many took part in the D-Day invasion of Normandy on June 6, 1944. Other soldiers were sent to the Pacific Theater to fight against the Japanese. Closer to home, however, soldiers trained for battle at Camp Edwards, a twenty-two-thousand-acre military training area. Camp Edwards was named for Clarence R. Edwards, the first commander of the Twenty-Sixth Yankee Division of the Massachusetts National Guard. Located on the Upper Cape, this military training facility was expanded during the beginning of the war to house the massive influx of training soldiers. During the height of construction in 1941, 18,343 workers were building 30 structures daily. It took 175 days to build an infrastructure of 1,300 buildings for the close to 30,000 soldiers who would come for basic training before being shipped out overseas.

Camp Edwards also housed the first German prisoners of war in barracks surrounded by stockades and barbed wire fences. The prisoners worked on

Cape Cod cranberry farms. According to a *Cape Cod Life* magazine article, from 1943 to 1946, some five thousand German soldiers were imprisoned at Camp Edwards. A mock German village was built for training exercises. The following glimpse into life for Cape Codders in World War II includes information on blackouts, rationing and victory gardens.

SERVICE SALUTE: A LOOK BACK TO WORLD WAR II ON CAPE COD

On August 6, 1942, the *Cape Cod Standard Times* published a "Service Salute." Since this was wartime, much of the day's edition was taken up with war news. The section largely comprised articles written by army wives and the activities planned by the United Service Organization (USO). Some of the headlines featured such stories as "Rationing Problems Vanquished by Resourceful Service Wife" and "Three New Books May Help Service Wives Pass the Time." Even the ads are oriented to the housewife: "Watch Junior devour our fresh home-made pies" from the Cape Cod Bakery in Hyannis.

One heartwarming story was revealed in an article about a British seaman, Leslie H. Hill, who visited his sister, Mrs. Alice White, of Hyannis Port. Hill saw active duty in Europe and then was sent to Nova Scotia and later visited the Cape. This was his first visit to the United States, and he had some interesting observations to make. When interviewed, he said the Cape reminded him of home. He noted that "in England, during wartime, no one over eight is allowed an orange and the fruit is for the most part non-existent as are bananas. Two eggs are the monthly quota." He also expressed relief that America had entered the war.

This is a fascinating look back in time but also a view of a country at war that we might find unfathomable. People's daily lives were shaped by the war effort. For example, on the front page of the *Cape Cod Standard Times* for August 6, 1942, one prominently placed article stated, "Headlight law violators fined." Apparently, the Massachusetts governor had ordered all car headlights to be half painted. People covered their windows and turned out lights during nightly blackouts so as not to be enemy targets. This war hit home in many ways—both small and large.

On the back page of this edition, under photos of Americans bombing Japan, there is a schedule for rationing. From meat and sugar to shoes, fuel oil and tires, Cape residents had to scrutinize every purchase. Finally, there was a pitch for "little gardens." With all food shipped overseas to feed hungry service men and women, Americans listened to the "voice of little gardens all over the country—millions of them in back yards, on lawns, in school house playgrounds, on former golf courses, wherever there is vacant land, there the earth will give of its fruits."

CAPE COD AFTER 1945

In later years, Cape Codders served in the Korean War, the Vietnam War, Operation Desert Storm and the 2003 Iraqi invasion. Both men and women served their country and came home to tell their stories. Many Cape towns have memorials that commemorate the fallen. In 1973, the U.S. Army began withdrawal from Camp Edwards, and the National Guard assumed control. The Otis Air Base became known as the Otis Air National Guard Base. When terrorists attacked the World Trade Center in New York City on September 11, 2001, F-15 fighter jets from Otis were the first to scramble in response.

A PAIR OF CAPE COD AUTHORS

Cape Cod's Storyteller, Joseph C. Lincoln

One of Cape Cod's most beloved and prolific writers was the larger-than-life author Joseph C. Lincoln, famous for his colorful, salty stories. He wrote many popular novels, including *Mary Gusta*, *Cap'n Eri* and *Keziah Coffin*. He wrote both poetry and novels in the purely Cape Cod vernacular. Many early visitors fell in love with Cape Cod through his books.

Joseph Crosby Lincoln was born in Brewster in February 13, 1870, son of Joseph Lincoln, a sea captain, and Emily (Crosby) Lincoln. He came from a long line of sea captains and was raised by his mother after his father died when he was one year old. His mother moved the family to Chelsea, Massachusetts, but maintained the family's Cape Cod summer home. When Lincoln came of age, his family decided he should become a businessman rather than ship out to sea as a cabin boy. Although he worked in a broker's office and a bank, the work didn't interest him, as he was an artistic boy and loved the outdoors. He studied drawing under the tutelage of Henry Sandman and eventually settled in Boston, where he began commercial art work. His love of the written word came into play when he started writing jingles to go along with his art. The new bicycle fad caught his interest, and he became associate editor of the *League of American Wheelmen Bulletin* in 1896. In 1899, he went to New York City to try his hand at writing. He sold his first story to the *Saturday Evening*

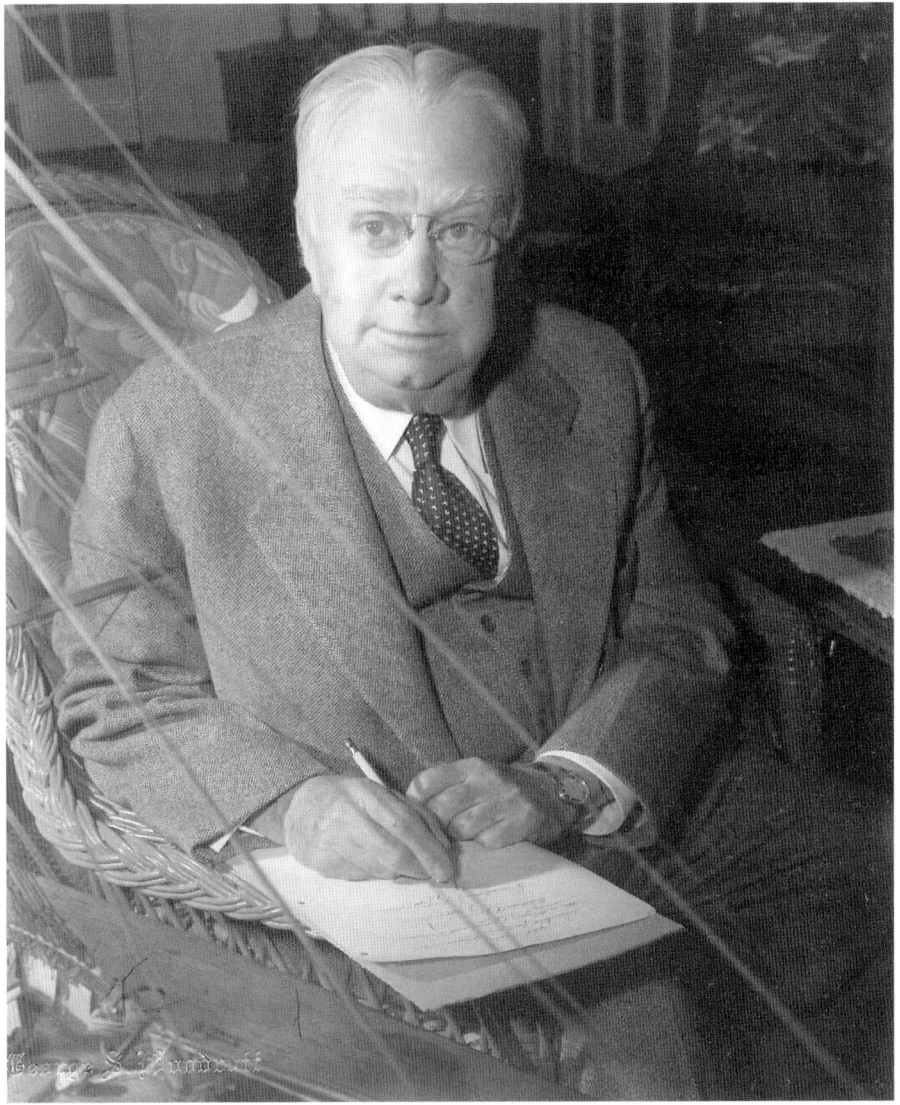

Photo of a seated Joseph Lincoln with pencil and pad of paper. *Courtesy the Chatham (MA) Historical Society.*

Post and became a regular contributor. It was around this time that he married Florence E. Sargent and later had a son, Freeman. The two would collaborate on books later in Lincoln's career.

His success with short stories led him to try a novel. His first novel, *Cap'n Eri*, was published in 1904 after he published a book of poems in 1902

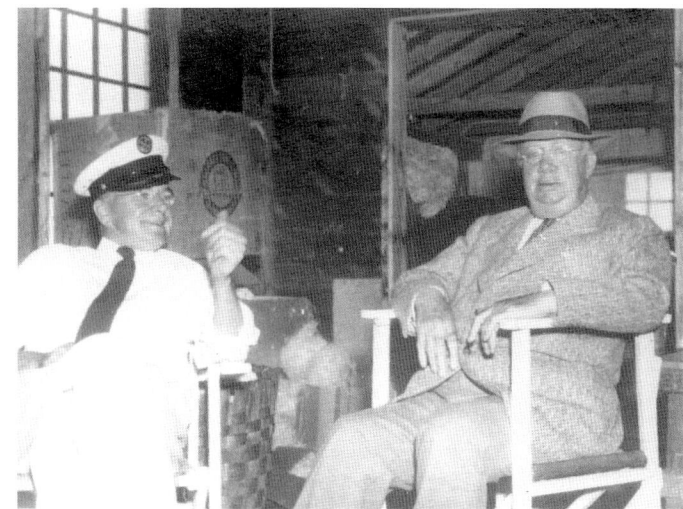

John Emery (owner of the Swinging Basket as well as the Sail Loft between 1938 and 1943) and Joseph C. Lincoln enjoying a friendly visit. *Courtesy the Chatham (MA) Historical Society.*

titled *Cape Cod Ballads*. Following his early success, he published at least one novel a year. He had a strict schedule for writing and worked from 9:30 a.m. to 12:30 p.m. every day. Working with plenty of yellow paper and a stubby pencil, he eschewed the practice of composing on a typewriter. In a 1938 *Cape Cod Standard Times* article, he described his method: "In any case, doing work that is satisfactory to me in any degree means I must fairly sweat over it." His characters included shopkeepers, old mariners and resourceful spinsters, with the locale as the "old fashioned, gossipy small town." There were romances, mysteries and family infighting, but in the end, the stories showed small towns and their inhabitants in a positive light.

When not writing books, he enjoyed sailing, golfing, motoring and visiting with friends. He also loved to read, including works by such authors as Rudyard Kipling, Mark Twain, Robert Louis Stevenson and Winston Churchill. Along with his family, he wintered in Philadelphia and summered in Chatham. His summer home, the Cross Trees, was located near the Chatham Bars Inn on Pleasant Bay. It became his family's summer home in 1917.

Lincoln's primary focus in his books was the ordinary Cape Codder. In a 1941 *Boston Herald* article, reporter Alice Dixon Bond wrote that Lincoln found his voice in writing about "the people of the little towns, sometimes inland, sometimes against the constant wash of the sea." When asked about his latest book, he said of his characters, "I've wanted to tell of people I've known. By that I don't mean that I draw my characters from life, for I most certainly do not…life contains both laughter and sorrow; and it seems to me

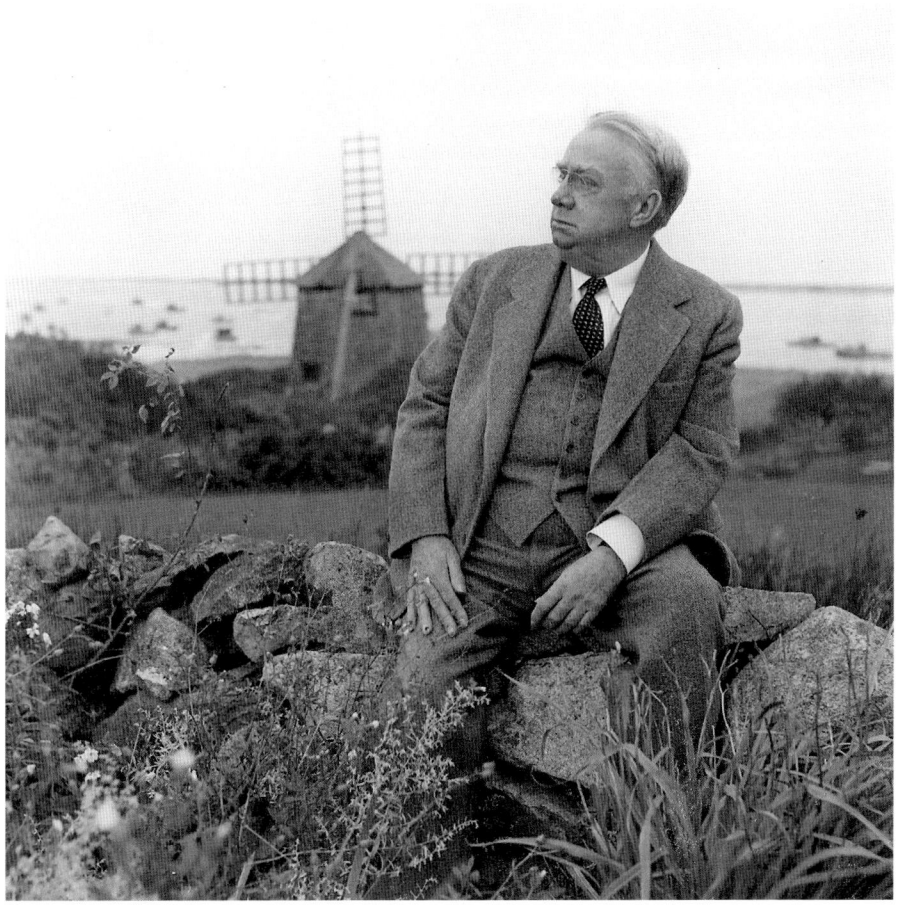

A photo of Joseph Lincoln seated in front of a windmill. *Courtesy the Chatham (MA) Historical Society.*

that the one is as real as the other. I have written of the average man for it is the average man who is the backbone of the nation."

Joseph Lincoln died on March 10, 1944, in his hotel suite in Winter Park, Florida. He produced forty-seven books in forty-two years, never once using a typewriter to write. At a testimonial dinner in his honor at the Copley Plaza Hotel in 1941, Dr. Claude M. Fuess, headmaster at Phillips Andover Academy, said of him, "I am distrustful of modern literature, but I find myself wanting to go back to honest villains and happy endings. Joe Lincoln offers these in his writings, together with a real breath of the clean salt air and sand of Cape Cod."

There is a Joseph Lincoln wing at the Chatham Historical Society, housed in the Atwood House & Museum, which contains manuscripts, first editions, illustrations and ephemera related to the author who made salty yarns come to life through his writings.

ROBERT NATHAN:
FAMOUS AUTHOR SUMMERED IN TRURO

The Cape is known for its many writers, artists and actors. There is also a New York–Provincetown connection, as many New York artists summer in Provincetown, as well as neighboring towns.

Many years ago, the novelist and poet Robert Nathan summered in Truro while spending his winters in New York City. He was most famous for his novels *The Bishop's Wife* and *Portrait of Jennie*, both made into award-winning films. Born in 1894 to a prominent Sephardic family, he was educated at Harvard, although he dropped out to take a job at an ad agency to support his family. During his lifetime, he had seven wives. He married his last wife, Anna Lee, in 1970.

Nathan had an affinity for Truro. His home, a former parsonage for Congregational ministers, was built in 1810. In fact, many of his books were written on Cape Cod, including the fantasy *Portrait of Jennie*. According to a 1942 *Cape Cod Standard Times* article, he collected old swords—a good choice, as he enjoyed fencing as well as golfing, swimming and sailing. He also liked to play the piano and sing. In his interview with Alice Dixon Bond (a former book critic for the *Boston Herald*), he talked about the writing process: "It is not insulation that is important to a creative artist, but the ability to keep part of your mind on the thing you are doing and yet be aware of the life that flows around you. I never shut myself away in a cocoon of my own making."

He had a long and prolific writing career. His first novel, *Peter Kindred*, was published in 1917, his last in 1975. Writing a novel every year or two, he wrote his drafts in longhand, revising day to day as he went along. Once he typed a draft, it was considered ready to go to the publisher's office. After a long, successful life, he died in Los Angeles in 1985 at the age of ninety-one.

As a summer visitor, Nathan enjoyed his quiet time in Truro. On May 14, 1942, he wrote a letter to the *Cape Cod Standard Times*. It was titled "Let Others Skulk, He Plans Return." The brief letter went: "Of course I will be on the Cape this summer—why not? And as a matter of fact, even earlier than usual. We want the good Cape air to blow the dismal winter out of our minds." In a short 1943 clip, Nathan described the Cape skies as "clear with stars and as dark and quiet as well water."

FAR-FLUNG CONNECTIONS

CAPE COD'S RUDYARD KIPLING CONNECTION

In 1897, the book *Captains Courageous*, a story of maritime adventure, was published. Its author, Rudyard Kipling, famous for such children's books as *The Jungle Book* and *Kim*, was born in Bombay, India, and felt ties with India for the rest of his life. As an adult, he lived for a time with his family in Brattleboro, Vermont, in an estate called the Naulahka. It was here where he met a former Cape Codder, Dr. James Conland. Although Conland was born in Brooklyn, New York, he lived part of his childhood in Chatham. After serving on ships from an early age, he came to the Cape with Elisha Morton Eldredge, who ran a grocery store between fishing seasons. Conland later shipped out to the Caribbean. It was these adventures that he would relate to Kipling in later years.

James Conland eventually married and settled down as a family doctor in Brattleboro. There he met Kipling, and the two became great friends. A 1983 *Cape Cod Times* article noted that Conland would "yarn to Kipling about witnessing open warfare there [Caribbean], of serving as cook and, by default when other crew members were down with the yellow fever, as second in command of a ship battling the Windward Passage between the islands of Haiti and Cuba." Conland helped deliver Kipling's oldest child during a snowstorm, and the two men "were regularly visiting over a sociable glass by the Kipling hearth, going on house calls together in the doctor's sleigh or buggy through the Vermont countryside."

The two even made trips to places like Gloucester or the Boston waterfront to "study the salty flavor of the busy port." These trips found their way into Kipling's *Captain Courageous*. There were many Cape Cod details in this famous book. Conland himself appears as Captain Troop, aboard the ship that Conland sailed in as a boy, the *Lucy Holmes*. The doctor's name appears on the title page in a simple dedication. On a sad note, Conland rushed to New York several years later to nurse Kipling and his oldest daughter. Both had come down with severe cases of lobar pneumonia. Kipling survived, but Josephine died. After this tragedy, Kipling put his Vermont house up for sale. Conland died of exhaustion in 1903 at the age of fifty-two. As Kipling later wrote about their longtime collaboration, "My part was the writing; his the details."

THE CAPE DUTCH CONNECTION

In July 1953, fifteen-year-old Princess Beatrix and her thirteen-year-old sister, Princess Irene, flew from the Netherlands to spend the summer in Chatham. Their hosts were the Feaver family of Ottawa; Mrs. Feaver was a school friend of Queen Juliana and Mr. Feaver was chief of protocol for Canada. It is interesting to note that during World War II, the Dutch royal family had escaped Europe in 1940 and stayed at the Canadian home of the Feavers, also spending time at a cottage at the Chatham Bars Inn. The princesses were no strangers to Cape Cod.

Their first course of action upon arriving in Chatham was to take a swim in a nearby pond. They were joined by their close friend, Renee, the Feavers' daughter. On July 18, 1953, there was a two-page article in the *Cape Cod Standard Times* complete with photos. The girls looked relaxed and athletic as they posed for photographers. The article stated that both girls were good riders and also loved to swim and sail. When asked about the American fashions, Princess Beatrix replied, "They don't have the shiny stones on dresses in Holland as you do in America." She continued by noting, "You American reporters ask a lot of questions. But we seldom see the answers we give you in the newspapers." The news article mentioned that Beatrix spoke French, Dutch and English.

The girls' father, Prince Bernhard, came for Princess Irene's fourteenth birthday in August. Selectmen from the town of Barnstable presented her with gifts. Selectman E. Thomas Murphy spoke: "Would you be so kind as to accept these little tokens, quite characteristic of Cape Cod, as an expression of our goodwill and friendliness." The princess would later send a thank-you note to the selectman for the presents chosen at Lorania's Toy Shop in Hyannis. The birthday girl attended "Call Me Madam" at the Cape Cod Music Circus. It was reported she got a "howl" out of the show and also met the famous songwriter, Irving Berlin, who was a member of the audience.

At the end of their visit, the girls visited Ottawa; meanwhile, Prince Bernhard escaped a near drowning while taking underwater pictures in the Caribbean shortly after his visit to Chatham. While doing some research on the royal family, I discovered that the royal family was again visiting the Cape in 1944 when a German U-boat sank off the coast of Cape Cod. Shortly after the announcement of the boat's sinking, the royal party departed for Canada. In the late 1980s, interest surfaced in raising the boat and unlocking its secrets.

On April 13, 2013, Queen Beatrix, age seventy-five, abdicated the throne after thirty-three years as ruler of the Netherlands and passed on her crown to her oldest son, Crown Prince Willem-Alexander, forty-five. He became the Netherlands' first king since Willem III died in 1890.

THE NEW YORK–CAPE COD CONNECTION

At the beginning of the twentieth century, artists began to flock to the Lower Cape and soon transformed the landscape. Budding writers and playwrights found the Cape's relaxed, artistic atmosphere welcoming and came in droves. In June 1916, the Provincetown Players opened its doors with Eugene O'Neill's first play, *Bound East for Cardiff*. Over the next few years, the theater grew, and the same group opened the first off-Broadway theater in New York. A thriving connection was established with actors, directors, writers and composers spending winters in New York and heading to Cape Cod in the summer. It was a perfect loop that served both locations.

Cape Cod was also a mecca for religious evangelicals, who came first to tent cities and later to small cottage colonies. According to the New England Historical Society, "tens of thousands of New Englanders went to religious revival camps in the summer to pray, preach and sing during the 19th century and well into the 20th century." The Craigville Conference Center began as a religious revival movement. South Wellfleet welcomed Methodists as early as 1819. Camp meetings also took place in Provincetown and Truro. In Oak

Bluffs on Martha's Vineyard, modern visitors are drawn to the gingerbread houses; the spot originated with Wesleyan Grove, where there were originally campground meeting tents.

New York businessmen also took advantage of the Cape's charms by bringing their families to Cape Cod at the beginning of the summer season and settling them into their summer homes. Many cottage colonies sprang up, and generations have grown up enjoying such activities as swimming, sunning and playing along Cape Cod beaches. On summer weekends, working fathers arrived by train, ferry, plane or car to spend weekends with their families. James O'Connell, in his book *Becoming Cape Cod: Creating a Seaside Resort*, wrote, "The introduction of the automobile led to the arrival of an increasing number of middle-class tourists, which in turn spawned proliferation of motels, inexpensive hotels, cottage colonies, and campsites."

EARLY IMMIGRANTS ON CAPE COD

Life on Cape Cod two hundred years ago was sometimes harsh and unforgiving. Early settlers had to find ways to support their families. In the eighteenth and nineteenth centuries, industries sprang up in unlikely places. Some of the early enterprises included tanning, salt works, glass works and cranberries. Of course, the Cape was perfect for fishing and offshore whaling. Small farms dotted the landscape. Windmills also helped early Cape Codders by providing power to salt works and to windmills for grinding flour.

Among the first immigrants to arrive were the Portuguese, coming from Portugal and the Azores to these shores. Many moved to Provincetown, where they became a major part of the fishing industry. A large number of Portuguese also moved to New Bedford to work in the whaling industry. According to a 2003 *Cape Cod Times* article, historian James Gould said of the Portuguese, "After the British, they were the oldest and biggest community." Many emigrated from the Cape Verde Islands seeking greater job opportunities. They became fishermen, farmers, whalers and workers in the cranberry bogs. In her book *Yesterday's Cape Cod*, author Evelyn Lawson wrote, "The Portuguese who had come in the middle 1800s were increasingly important to the social, economic, and cultural life of the lower Cape."

The Irish also moved to Cape Cod hoping to find a hospitable place to make a life. In her book *Harwich*, author Joan M. Maloney wrote that the Irish were early immigrants to Harwich. She asserted that although they were "welcomed for their labor, they often encountered hostility because of

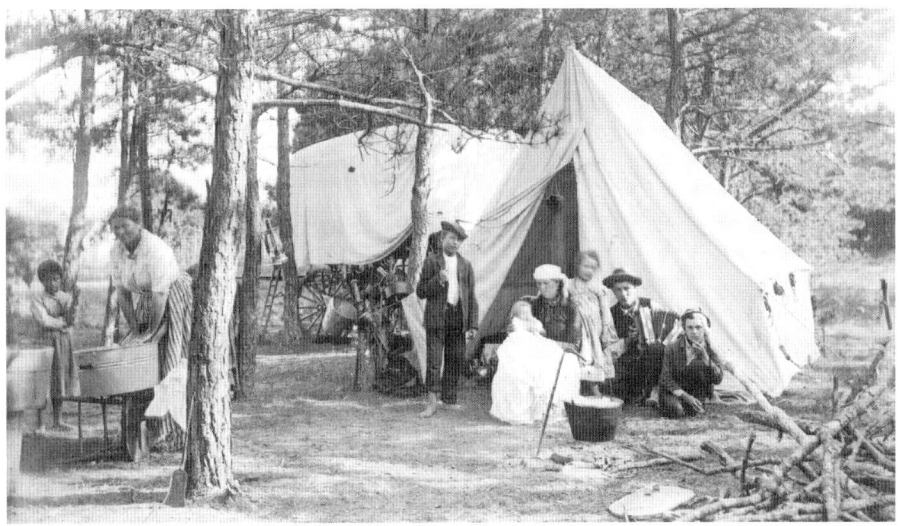

A family of gypsies or itinerant workers in front of a tent. *Courtesy of the W.B. Nickerson Archives, Cape Cod Community College.*

their religion." The first Catholic church in Harwich was built in the mid-1850s, with the priest traveling from Sandwich to serve worshipers from neighboring towns. The Irish spirit stills flourishes on Cape Cod, with its numerous Irish pubs and restaurants.

In West Barnstable, a number of Finnish immigrants came in the late nineteenth and early twentieth century. In fact, the eastern part of that village is sometimes called "Finn Town." A 2007 *Cape Cod Times* article about Finnish descendants noted that "dozens of Finnish families settled in Falmouth, West Yarmouth and Barnstable.…[T]hey came for cranberries. They worked in the West Barnstable brickyard and the Keith CarWorks in Sagamore." They brought their traditions and their love of family to a new land.

In more recent years, people from other countries have settled on the Cape, including Brazilians and Jamaicans. According to the 2010 census, there are sixty-eight thousand Brazilian immigrants in Massachusetts, many of them living on Cape Cod. The goal of many Brazilians has been to find better job opportunities and earn money to send back to family living in Brazil. Overall, this influx of immigrants has enriched Cape Cod over the past few centuries.

SANDWICH'S HISTORIC PAST

THE WINGS OF CAPE COD

The Wing family, one of the original Cape families, moved to Sandwich in the 1600s. They were among the first Cape settlers and one of the ten founding families of Sandwich. The Wing House was constructed in 1641 and is said to be one of the oldest houses in New England. It was originally known as Fort House and was possibly a refuge from Indian attack in its early days. The first Wing to live in the house was Stephen Wing, who moved there in 1646. He and his brother Daniel, from a family that included four sons, were among the earliest converts to the Quaker faith. Later, more than sixty Wings fought during the Revolutionary War.

The Wing Family of America bought the house in 1942 from the last Wing resident. In an effort to preserve the deteriorating family home, the Wings opened it as a public museum. Visitors can view seven rooms furnished with antique household items. Many of these pieces have been donated by family members. There is a Keeping Room with a huge fireplace where the family members cooked and ate. One highlight is the eighteenth-century room with Stephen Wing's original desk and chair.

Chauncy Phelps Wing originated the idea for a family reunion around 1880, when he compiled a family genealogy. The home is now the setting for annual Wing family reunions, and the family has been meeting continuously since 1902. For that first reunion, one hundred descendants came by horse

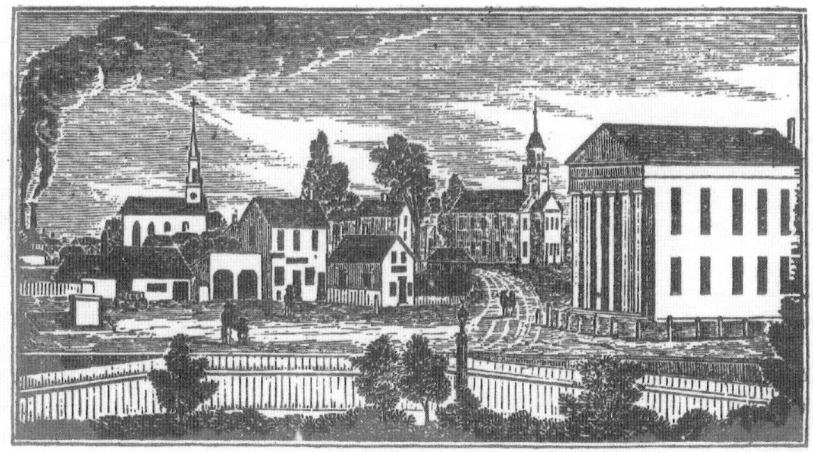

Western view of Sandwich, (central part).

A vintage postcard depicting a view of the western part of Sandwich. *From the postcard collection of Wendell E. Smith.*

and buggy to the Cape. Sandwich's tax collector of that time, Peleg Brown, was presented with thirty pounds of butter in a wheelbarrow (a symbolic celebration of their payment of taxes). This became known as the "Butter Parade" and was often reenacted in later reunions.

Family members come from all over the United States and England for the reunion. In fact, there are 1,200 dues-paying members in the Wing Family of America organization.

QUAKER BURIAL GROUND

In 1694, the town of Sandwich gave to its "neighbors called Quakers, half an acre of ground for a burial place on the hill above the Canoe Swamp and between the 'Ways' at Spring Hill." According to capecodquakers.org, Sandwich has the oldest continuous meeting in America. The first meeting took place on April 13, 1657, at the home of William and Priscilla Allen at Spring Hill, East Sandwich. These early Quakers were persecuted and even jailed for holding illegal meetings. Later meetings formed in Yarmouth and Falmouth. All three towns now have active Quaker communities.

When Edward Perry, an early Quaker, died in 1695, there was no stone to mark his grave. It was the practice at that time to bury Quakers in unmarked graves. Perry was one of the first settlers of the town of Bourne and the first known clerk of the meeting. He was often called "Edward, the Quaker." The first burial in Falmouth occurred in 1685. This is the oldest recorded Quaker burial on Cape Cod.

The Sandwich meeting was known for its high rate of literacy and female equality. In 1709, a second meetinghouse was built in what is now South Yarmouth. Then, in 1720, West Falmouth became the next site for a meetinghouse. As of this writing, the oldest extant building is the South Yarmouth meetinghouse, built in 1808. The present Sandwich meetinghouse was built in 1810 (and was the third to be built for the Sandwich Quakers). The currently used Falmouth meetinghouse was built in September 1842. In 1888, many of the old boulders used to mark graves were replaced by headstones.

Sandwich's Famous Antique Glass

Few people think of Cape Cod as being a thriving industrial area, but many industries have grown up and flourished here. In particular, the Boston & Sandwich Glass Company offered employment for many Cape Codders. In 1825, a Boston businessman, Deming Jarves, chose Sandwich for his glass-making company. He was attracted by its pine forests, its proximity to water and its accessibility to sand. Also, there was ample local labor to sweeten the deal. He bought two thousand acres of land and brought skilled glassmakers (called "gaffers") from overseas. He later discovered that the Cape sand wasn't suitable for his glassmaking business, so he had to haul sand from Morris River, New Jersey, the Berkshires and even from France and British Guiana.

The Boston & Sandwich Glass Company and its offshoots changed the nature of Sandwich. Although its citizens were descendants of the original settlers who arrived in the 1600s, many of the glass workers were imported from England and Ireland because there were no native glassblowers in this area. In her book *Earning a Living on Olde Cape Cod*, author Marion Vuilleumier wrote, "These men blew intricate glass pieces and trained the first local workers. The elite employees at the factory were the glass blowers, and they let every one else know it." When patented molds were

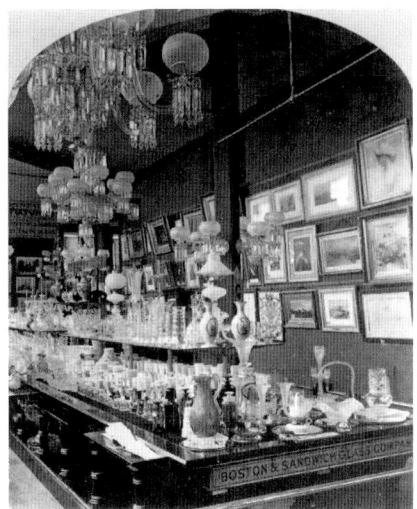 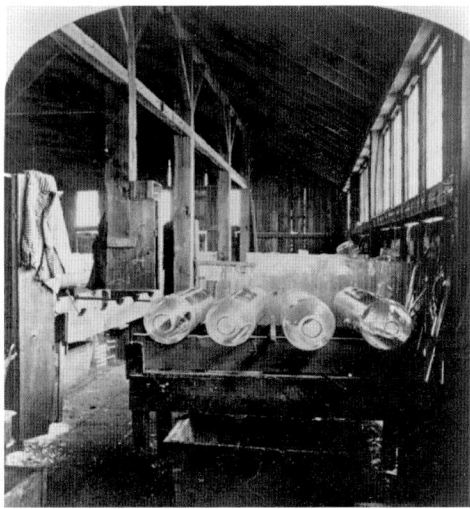

Left: A display of Sandwich glass featuring a wide range of rare glass from the local Boston & Sandwich Glass Factory, founded in 1825. *Courtesy of the W.B. Nickerson Archives, Cape Cod Community College.*

Right: Glass tubes from the Boston & Sandwich Glass Factory. *Courtesy of the W.B. Nickerson Archives, Cape Cod Community College.*

introduced by Jarves, the master craftsmen were unhappy, and Jarves received several death threats. The goal was to mass-produce glassware that would not be taxed so heavily. At its height, the company employed six hundred people.

During the nineteenth century, the factory flourished, although Jarves often feuded with his investors. Then, in 1858, the company began showing less profit, so Jarves took his son, John W. Jarves, and started a new company down the road: the Cape Cod Glass Works. Unfortunately, the younger Jarves died in 1863, after which his seventy-five-year-old father started losing interest in the family business.

The glass works' furnaces were stopped on the same day that Deming Jarves died in 1869. The Cape Cod Glass Works was taken over by John Charles DeVoy, who had an interest in making variegated colored glass (or vasa murrhina). This is also called "spangled" or "spattered" glass. The last company to try its luck was the Alton Manufacturing Company in 1907. During the early part of the twentieth century, the glass making industry died out, and little remained of the original factory buildings by the 1940s.

In 1907, the Sandwich Historical Society was founded and held its first glass exhibit in 1925. It was decided to permanently house the glass collection in the Sandwich Glass Museum. According to its website (www.sandwichglassmuseum.org), the collection holds more than five thousand pieces produced between 1825 and 1888, including paperweights, lamps, cut glass and hand-decorated pieces. Thanks to the vision of one man, this part of Cape history can be shared and enjoyed by residents and visitors alike.

RIPTIDE DISASTER

AUGUST 22, 1973

On a beautiful August day, when scores of people played in the surf at Nauset Beach in Orleans and hundreds more enjoyed the sun on the shore, a terrifying event occurred shortly after 11:30 a.m. There had been recent rough seas, and an offshore riptide began to drag swimmers straight out to sea. In a news account in the *Cape Cod Standard Times*, an eyewitness recounted that it was "like a tornado in the water, it just sucked you in." It was thought that swimmers were attracted by a low tide, just before it turned to come in and caught them by surprise.

Lifeguards, aided by several unidentified swimmers, "braved a sudden and treacherous riptide to drag more than 30 persons from the Atlantic Ocean to safety." Earlier in the day, lifeguards had warned an estimated two hundred people in the water to go no deeper than their waists. Some lost their footing when the riptide struck. Five lifeguards were on duty on the estimated six-hundred-yard-long beach. Assistant lifeguard Lee Anderson of South Easton made the first rescue. He saved a young boy and gave him mouth-to-mouth resuscitation. A couple was rescued by chief lifeguard Gary Guertin of Attleboro, who had help from another lifeguard, Aldo Ghisalbelt of Dobbs Ferry, New York. Nineteen-year-old David O'Brien of Orleans later said that he and his coworkers used torpedo buoys to bring swimmers to safety. The fifth lifeguard at the center of the action was Michael Coughlan of Wilmington, Delaware.

Assistance from many surrounding towns brought rescue squads and ambulances quickly to the scene. Mutual aid came from Eastham, Brewster

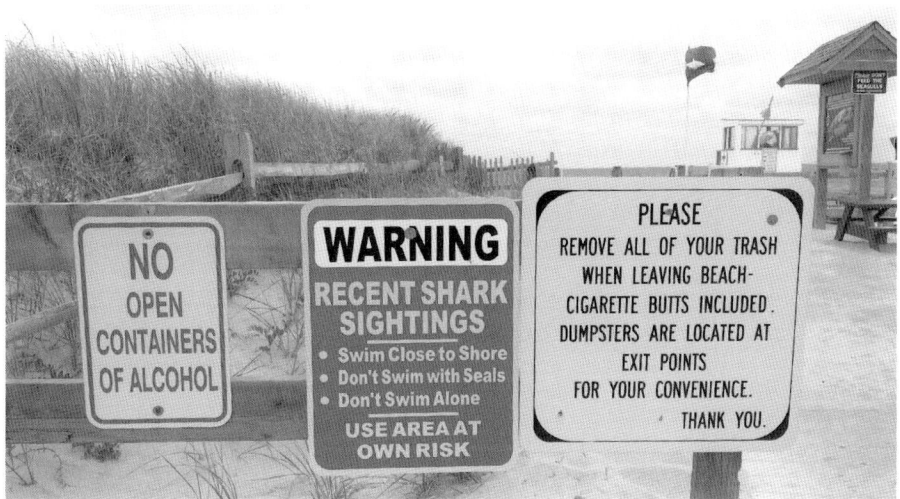

Beach warning signs at Nauset Beach, Orleans. *Courtesy of Cynthia Sherrick Mitchell.*

and Chatham. Police cruisers, fire-rescue personnel and two helicopters from the Coast Guard base at Otis were dispatched to aid rescue operations. Fourteen of those rescued were brought in relays to Cape Cod Hospital, with one in intensive care and seven others hospitalized. It was reported that a Melrose woman drowned and was the only known fatality.

Orleans police chief Chester A. Landers described the near-disaster as "totally unexpected. In all my 20 odd years here, nothing like this has ever happened." It was reported that a "human chain" of some "30 people was formed in an unguarded section of the beach, but the surf broke the chain and tossed 15 people back into the sea. All were saved." It was a harrowing scene and one that beachgoers that day would remember for years to come.

One former resident, Laurie Smith Murphy, then living in East Orleans and eighteen years old at the time, remembered that day. She said when it was apparent that swimmers in the water were in danger, the call went out for volunteers to help form "human chains." Murphy recalled that the volunteers were told to stand facing in opposite directions, as it would make their grip stronger and the chain harder to break. She said she and her friends were at the left end of the beach so they could watch the surfers. What she remembered most clearly was the aftermath of that day. The beach was closed the following day, and Laurie can still call to mind how eerie and quiet it was. "It felt empty," she said. "It's not something I will ever forget."

Nowadays, there is more public awareness about riptides and the danger they can pose to the unwary swimmer. The key to surviving a riptide, if you can't swim out of it, is to float on your back and allow the riptide to take you away from shore until you are beyond the pull of the current. Then you can swim safely back to shore. Many beaches now put up warning posters alerting swimmers to the possibility of riptides, especially if the seas are rough.

ORLEANS

A TOWN WITH HISTORY

Orleans is often called the "hub of the Lower Cape." It is a thriving town for business and tourism, with such attractions as the French Cable Museum and Academy Playhouse. It also boasts attractive beaches such as Skaket Beach (on the bay side) and Nauset Beach (on the ocean side). The town was named in honor of Louis Phillipe II, Duke of Orleans. It is the only town on Cape Cod whose name is not taken from English or Indian origins. Here, then, is a collection of some Orleans highlights.

WHAT WAS JEREMIAH'S GUTTER?

The quick answer is that Jeremiah's Gutter was a canal in Orleans and the first Cape Cod canal. A "gutter" was the historic name for a storm-made "cut" that channeled across the peninsula from Cape Cod Bay over what is now Route 6 in Orleans into Town Cove. It was also called Jeremiah's Dream, with "dream" a play on the word "drain."

Jeremiah Smith, member of a pioneer Eastham family dating back to 1655, was the man associated with the early canal attempt because he was the adjacent property owner. The great storm of 1717 made a passage of sorts over land from the Orleans Town Cove to Eastham's Boat Meadow Creek. There were efforts to close this up, although it allowed a whaleboat to pass from the bay to the ocean.

Then, in 1804, a canal was first dug over this periodically flooding lowland—much of it the property of Jeremiah Smith. It was also used as an escape route by local boatmen in the War of 1812. The canal remained passable until 1817. By 1844, heavy ocean tides were crashing over the land and creating a natural channel between the lower and mid parts of the Cape. During his time on Cape Cod, Henry David Thoreau is said to have forded the gutter.

Not many visible remains are left to mark this site. Still, it is interesting to note that Cape Cod's first canal was in a completely different location than it is now.

SNAPSHOT OF ROCK HARBOR

Rock Harbor in the early 1900s was a simple tidal pool that has since been opened up and deepened into a major commercial port and recreational fishing port serving Cape Cod Bay. A line of young pine trees marks the narrow boat channel out to the bay. In fact, new markers are planted every year at the beginning of the summer season to aid in navigation going in and out of the harbor.

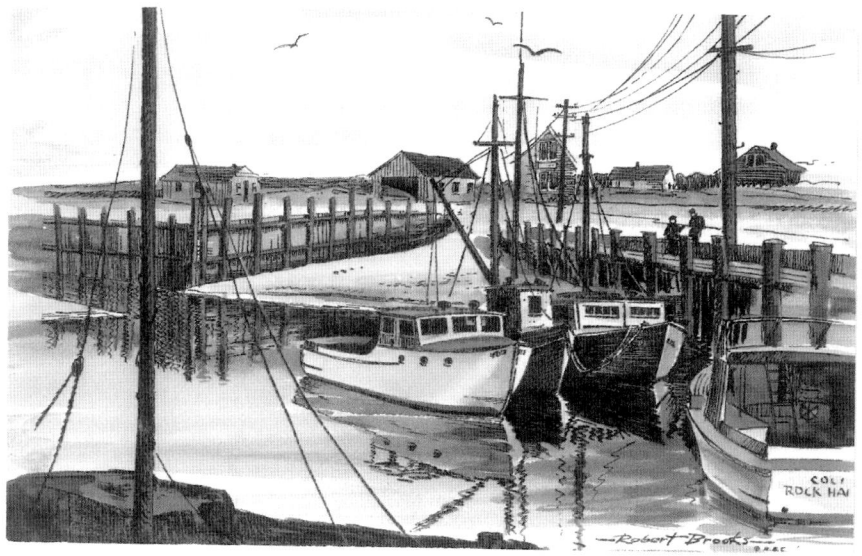

Boats at Rock Harbor from a postcard by artist Robert Brooks. *From the postcard collection of Wendell E. Smith.*

During the War of 1812, the harbor hosted a battle between the British marines and local militia. The British were blockading towns all up and down Cape Cod. The attack on Rock Harbor occurred in December 1814 by British marines from HMS *Newcastle*. The British suffered one fatality.

Shortly thereafter, according to Daniel Lombardo in his book *Orleans*, "In 1814, the town built a landing there and a road connecting the harbor to the town. At that time, packet ships transported goods between Orleans and Boston. Thus, for many years the town's shipping business was centered at Rock Harbor."

As is fitting, Rock Harbor is named after the rocks at the entrance of the harbor. Small boats and fishing vessels are moored here, and the place is a center of activity and fun. It's a spot to seek out a charter boat for a day of fishing or watch the spectacular sunsets.

MAYO'S DUCK FARM

In the 1960s, families often went to Mayo's Duck Farm for dinner. Long tables were set up outside and laden with food. Visitors ate picnic-style in the fresh air, with plates piled high with chicken, mashed potatoes, corn on the cob and delicious squash muffins. Afterward, diners often drove to Nauset Beach to listen to concerts at the gazebo.

Mayo's Duck Farm was started by Walter Mayo in 1895 and was first called the Nauset Poultry Farm. According to capecodweb.com, the farm was producing fifty thousand ducklings in 1918. The venture was hugely successful and later became a restaurant and catering business. The business closed its doors in 1968.

In a faded 1947 *Cape Cod Standard Times* news clip, an endearing story emerges of nine-year-old Walter "Ducky" Mayo, who wrote a letter to Princess Elizabeth. When a letter arrived in response to his, the young boy showed it off to neighbors and friends and then carefully placed it in his scrapbook. The letter read, in part: "Buckingham Palace. The Lady-in-waiting is desired by the Princess Elizabeth to thank Master Walter Mayo for his kind message on the occasion of the announcement of Her Royal Highness' engagement." The article mentioned Walter's busy summers working at the Duck Farm owned and operated by his father and grandfather. In one week, he reportedly took 12,500 chickens out of their incubators.

Twenty years after "Ducky" Mayo wrote his letter, he went on to have an illustrious career. Walter H. Mayo III received a BA degree at Trinity College in Hartford in 1959, majoring in both government and history. He graduated from Yale University Law School in 1962 and was later appointed as the Massachusetts assistant attorney general by Attorney General Elliott Richardson in 1967. It all started at Mayo's Duck Farm.

MARSH PEOPLE AND PUKWUDGIES

MARSH PEOPLE

Cape Cod has many natural wonders, including beaches, sand dunes and kettle ponds formed by glaciers. It is also home to salt marshes—lovely and sometimes lonely areas that are home to birds, fishes and shellfish. Legends have grown up around the marshes, including stories of strange creatures living in or about the Great Marsh that runs from Sandwich to Yarmouth. The "Marsh People"—if they are real—are supposedly the descendants of long-ago villagers who fled the stifling strictures of life in Puritan New England.

One local paranormal investigator, Derek Bartlett—founder of and president of the Cape and Islands Paranormal Research Society (CAIPRS)—described these beings as "human-like creatures" who have reportedly been seen in many marshes along the Cape. He maintains that duck hunters have claimed to encounter them in the Great Marsh and also tells the story of kayakers who disappeared, never to be seen again. It is not only people who have reportedly vanished there but also horses and other animals.

Another author and investigator of paranormal happenings is Jeff Belanger. According to his website (legendtripping.com), he has interviewed thousands of alleged eyewitnesses to such occurrences. In a 2010 article published on his website, Belanger conducted a lengthy interview with Derek Bartlett. He reported that Bartlett spent one April evening in 2002

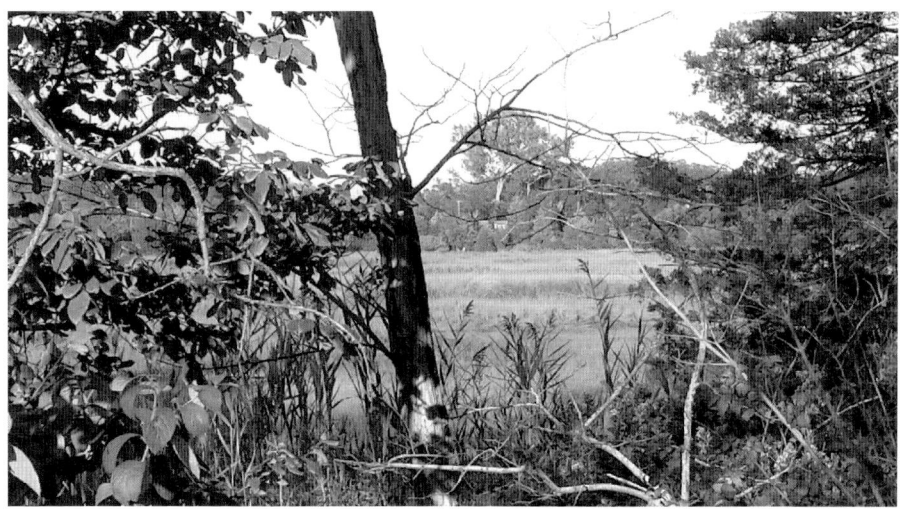

Shot of a Cape Cod marsh. *Courtesy of Cynthia Sherrick Mitchell.*

watching the marsh. Bartlett's strange tale went like this: "I would watch the marsh with my scope. I saw what appeared to be people walking, but it wasn't on the railroad tracks that cut through the middle. It was beyond that. I stood and watched and watched. They were very light and then they vanished. It was high tide. They weren't in a canoe. They were walking. I saw the movement of walking and then they were gone."

Interestingly, Bartlett described the phantom walkers as "light," whereas other reports talk of the Marsh People as "dark as the mud." In a 2013 *Cape Cod Times* article, Barlett discussed an account from 1814 about a farmer in West Barnstable who reported creatures coming out of the marsh, "grabbing onto his full-size horse and dragging it back in. He described these creatures as being three feet in height, very skinny-looking and [having] skin color as dark as the marsh mud—very, very dark."

Reports have persisted over centuries of something lurking in the marshy depths. Although these creatures may appear malevolent, perhaps they only want to be left alone.

THE "LITTLE PEOPLE" OR PUKWUDGIES

The Wampanoag of southern New England have many legends about mystical creatures, but none so fascinating as that of the "little people" or Pukwudgies. These two- to three-foot beings were sometimes described as smooth, gray and smelling of flowers—but also as being hairy-faced and having horns. They had oversized noses and long grasping fingers. The name literally translates to "little wild man of the woods that vanishes." Like the Marsh People, there were conflicting reports of their activities, for good and for evil.

It is thought the Pukwudgies were originally helpful to the Wampanoag, but the native peoples aligned with the creator giant Maushop and his wife, Granny Squannit. According to Native American folklore, Maushop was believed to have created much of Cape Cod, as well as the islands of Nantucket and Martha's Vineyard. In retaliation for this perceived betrayal, the little people began to play mischievous and sometimes devious tricks on the Indians. Some stories related that the Pukwudgies killed Maushop's sons with arrows; in response, he retreated in his grief.

The Pukwudgies have many supernatural traits, such as appearing and disappearing, luring people to their deaths and creating fire at will. Several suicides in the Freetown–Fall River Forest in Massachusetts, people leaping from Assonet Ledge, have been pointed to as the work of the fierce "little people." Stories have been written about the Bridgewater Triangle, with the towns of Abington, Freetown and Rehoboth forming the corners of the triangle. Rehoboth, established in 1643, is one of the oldest towns in Massachusetts. Along with the Pukwudgies, the Bridgewater Triangle area has supposedly been the site of paranormal activity, including encounters with ghosts and orbs, as well as UFO and Bigfoot sightings. Some paranormal experts consider all of southeastern Massachusetts to be part of this area.

One sinister myth involves the Pukwudgies controlling the so-called Tei-pai-Wankas, which are said to be the souls of the people they have killed. The Wampanoag believe that it is best to leave the Pukwudgies alone. If you are walking in the forest, beware of the shape-shifting, mischievous "little people" and don't say their name out loud. Like the fairies, elves and gnomes that reside in Europe, the Pukwudgies are magical beings not to be tampered with.

CAPE COD INSTITUTIONS

CAPE COD FIVE: A BANK WITH A LONG HISTORY

One bank has a particularly interesting past. The Cape Cod Five Cents Savings Bank was incorporated in Harwich in 1855 as a state-chartered mutual savings bank. Depositers could open an account with as little as five cents (hence the name of the customer-friendly bank). The first deposit was made by John Burk on April 29, 1856, when the first branch opened in Orleans at the store of H.K. Cummings. At present, there are twenty branches from Wellfleet to Mashpee, as well as branches in Wareham, Vineyard Haven and Nantucket.

The first president was Nathan Underwood, who served one year. Later, a series of Snows took over the helm, with Nathaniel Snow becoming the second president of the bank and serving until 1871. His portrait was unveiled in 1956. Next, Augustus C. Snow served as chairman of the board from 1904 until his death in 1919. When Ralph B. Snow was elected bank president in 1952, he succeeded his father, Ralph H. Snow. His was the third generation of Snows connected to the bank. The Snow line was broken when Elliott Carr became Cape Cod Five Cents Savings Bank's president in 1982.

Over the years, the bank has marked many milestones. In 1955, the bank celebrated its 100th birthday with fanfare. At that time, there were only ten employees; now, there are more than 350. Then, in 1990, Cape Cod Five committed $5 million for affordable housing loans. In that same year, the Dolphin Branch opened at Dennis-Yarmouth High School as a school-business partnership. Later, the bank had a banner year in 1993 when it posted record earnings of $8.03 million. It became the largest Cape-based bank, surpassing Cape Cod Bank & Trust Company.

Cape Cod Five joined the internet age when it began offering internet banking in 1998. It had earlier launched credit and debit cards in 1995 for its customers. In June 2004, the bank announced that bank president Elliot Carr would step down. His replacement was Dorothy A. Savarese, the bank's first female president and its eighteenth president overall. On October 31, 2017, the bank celebrated the groundbreaking for a $45 million headquarters project on Route 132 in Hyannis.

The bank remains "defiantly independent"—operating as a mutual trust, with no stockholders. Nickels, dimes or pennies—it's nice to know there's a piece of the 1800s still flourishing today.

CELEBRATING THE FAIR

Each July, the Barnstable County Fair returns to celebrate everything Americana from cotton candy to carnival rides, games and livestock. There are both adult and youth exhibits, with judging for flower arrangements, homemade baked goods and gigantic vegetables, photography and clothing to name a few. The quilting exhibition is popular and a must-see for many fairgoers. Over in the Youth Hall, kids can win ribbons for crafts, paintings and drawings.

How did this annual event get its start? In October 1844, the Barnstable County Agricultural Society held its first fair at the county courthouse complex in Barnstable Village. In the early years, popular events included trotting horses, sulky races and vaudeville acts, as well as Grange and livestock exhibits. It's fun to imagine women in long skirts, boys in boots and breeches, girls with pinafores and bonnets and men in frock coats traversing the fields to catch a show or sample a piece of prize-winning cake. In earlier days, there was a much-anticipated Children's Day.

In 1899, the Agricultural Ball was the highlight of the fair. The fair website recalled past activities, including "the gaily-trimmed Exhibition Hall, where ladies and gentleman in evening finery danced to the music of Brigham's eight-piece band." By 1920, the Agricultural Society had erected a $2,500

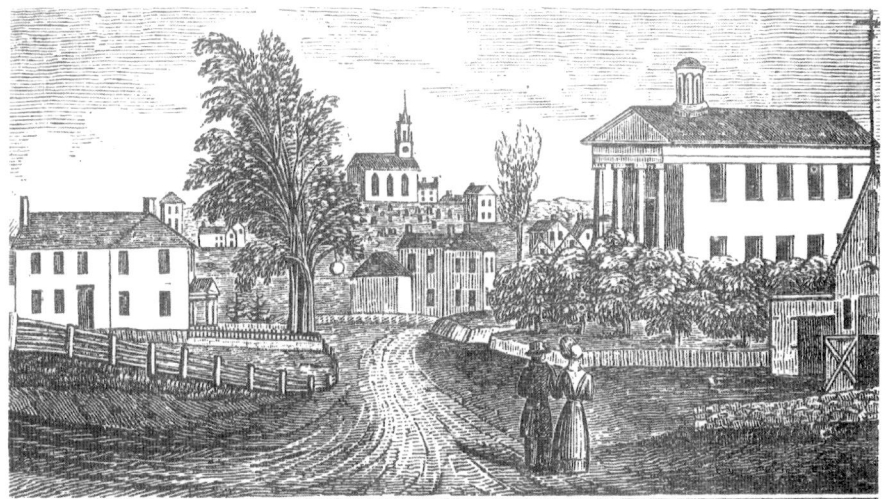

North western view of the Barnstable Court-House, and other buildings.

An antique postcard of the Barnstable County Courthouse. *From the postcard collection of Wendell E. Smith.*

poultry building and spent $1,500 on paint. But by 1931, as the country entered the Great Depression, the fair was losing money. It was decided to suspend operations. Not until 1954 did the modern-day reintroduction of the county fair appear (although attempts were made in 1932 and 1939). The project almost didn't get off the ground in 1955, after a polio scare and hurricane had the fair opening and closing on the same day. In the spring of 1973, the fair was moved from Marstons Mills to its present location in East Falmouth.

The magic of the fair continues despite parking woes, hot weather and occasional noise complaints. There have been diverse events, such as the horse pulling contest in 1993, a dog show in 1994, a pig race in 1996 and the twenty-two-ton sand sculpture of a seaside castle created by artist Justin Gordon in 1995, as well as shows by such performers as the Kingston Trio, the Fifth Dimension, Chuck Mangione and the Marshall Tucker Band, to name a few. Kids can enjoy the Midway with its many rides and games. This annual event is one that locals and tourists can enjoy on a hot July day.

THE PROUD TRADITION OF TOWN MEETINGS

The tradition of attending town meetings is unique to small towns in New England. It is a form of direct democratic rule. The first town meetings, an early form of self-government, were introduced in Massachusetts shortly after the Puritans arrived here. Other American institutions introduced to the state were newspapers and the first private academies.

The meetinghouse was the place where town meetings were held 350 years ago. During Puritan times, participation was restricted to male property holders who were also church members. Those who failed to appear were fined. By 1776, the town clerk was empowered to call town meetings to elect selectmen if a majority of the selectmen had moved from town or were absent while in service to their country.

One reason why Massachusetts colonists revolted against Great Britain was the British attempt to ban most town meetings except by permission. In 1774, British soldiers tried to stop a Salem town meeting in progress, but early Americans were determined to keep their freedom, so the citizens barred the door of their townhouses and continued their meeting.

Another example of an early town meeting occurred on the first day of fighting during the American Revolution. Members of the Lexington militia gathered on the town common at about 2:00 a.m. on April 19, 1775. There they held an impromptu town meeting to "consult what might be done" about the British soldiers marching from Boston. The rest of the story is history.

The proud tradition of holding town meetings still prevails on Cape Cod. Towns across the Cape will hold their annual spring town meetings to approve a budget for the upcoming year. Towns with more than six thousand residents have a representative town meeting system. As Alexis de Tocqueville stated in his *Democracy in America*, "Town meetings are to liberty what public schools are to science: they bring [government] within the people's reach, they teach men how to use and how to enjoy it."

TONY COSTA MURDERS

In the winter of 1969, the women of Truro were afraid. In February, the mutilated body of a girl was discovered in a shallow grave there. In this tightknit community, murders were rare, and a discovery this horrific was unthinkable. Then, on March 5, the dismembered bodies of two young women who had been reported missing earlier were also found in a shallow grave. In a *Cape Cod Standard Times* article, Aldred K. Souza, a Truro resident, was quoted as saying, "The whole thing has people nervous; my wife, Pat, and other women are extremely apprehensive. We live only one-half mile from where the bodies were found, and have to stop and think about this guy roaming around the area. I saw part of the last body, and it wasn't pleasant."

What or who was responsible for the deaths? The two women whose bodies were discovered together were from Providence, Rhode Island. Patricia Walsh was a schoolteacher at the Laurel Hill Elementary School in Providence, while Mary Ann Wysocki was a junior at Rhode Island College. Both girls had been good friends since they attended Classical High School in Providence together. They left home on January 24 to spend the weekend in Provincetown. After checking into a rooming house at 5 Standish Street, owned by Mrs. Patricia Morton, they left there together on January 25 and were not seen alive again. Since the girls had paid their rent in advance and left early in the morning, the landlady was not alarmed. But on the following Monday, both of the girls' parents filed a missing person's report.

Before the girls were reported as missing, the blue Volkswagen driven by Patricia Walsh was spotted at the National Seashore on January 25. A note on the dashboard stated the car had broken down and the driver had

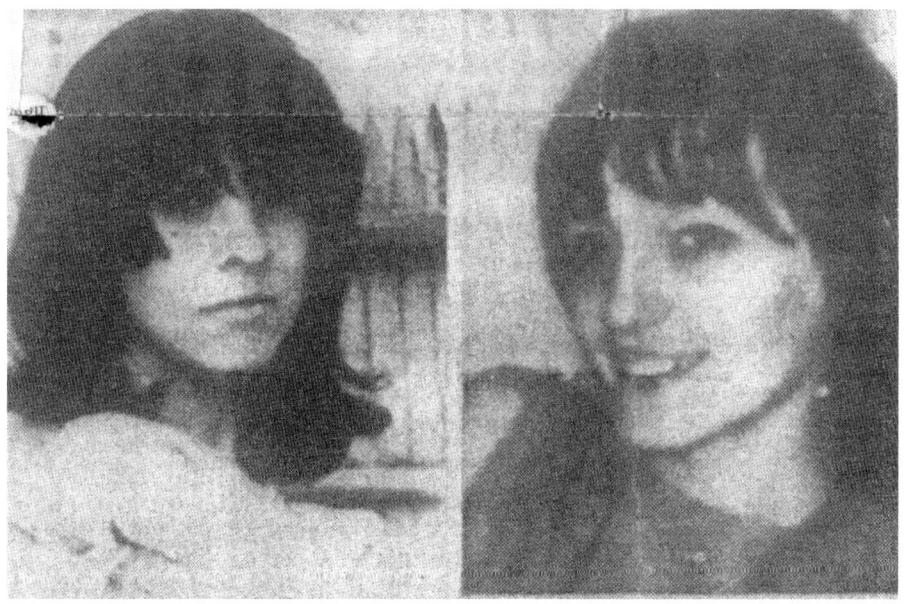

A newspaper photo of Tony Costa's victims, Patricia Walsh and Mary Ann Wysocki, circa 1969. *Special to the* Cape Cod Standard Times.

gone for assistance. Later, on February 10, the car was found in a parking lot in Burlington, Vermont. The owner of the lot told police detectives that Antone C. Costa of Provincetown had paid a week's parking fee. Costa was questioned by detectives the day the car was found. He told them he had bought the car from Patricia Walsh. When the car was impounded, however, a spot of blood was discovered in the back seat.

Search crews spent twenty-five days searching the area where the earlier body was found. The search was headed by Lieutenant George Killen, detective at the District Attorney's Office of Barnstable County. The area, about a mile and a half from the old Truro Cemetery, was heavily wooded, with thick underbrush. Recent rains had impeded the search, but a rope was found that led to the discovery of the shallow grave with the dismembered remains of Walsh and Wysocki, as well as a third body that had been there longer and was badly decomposed. Each body was "cut into as many parts as there are joints." There were also reports of teeth marks on different dismembered parts. It was first reported that the girls' hearts were missing, but this turned out to be erroneous.

Following autopsies, it was announced that the Providence women had died from gunshot wounds. There were two bullets in Mary Ann Wysocki's

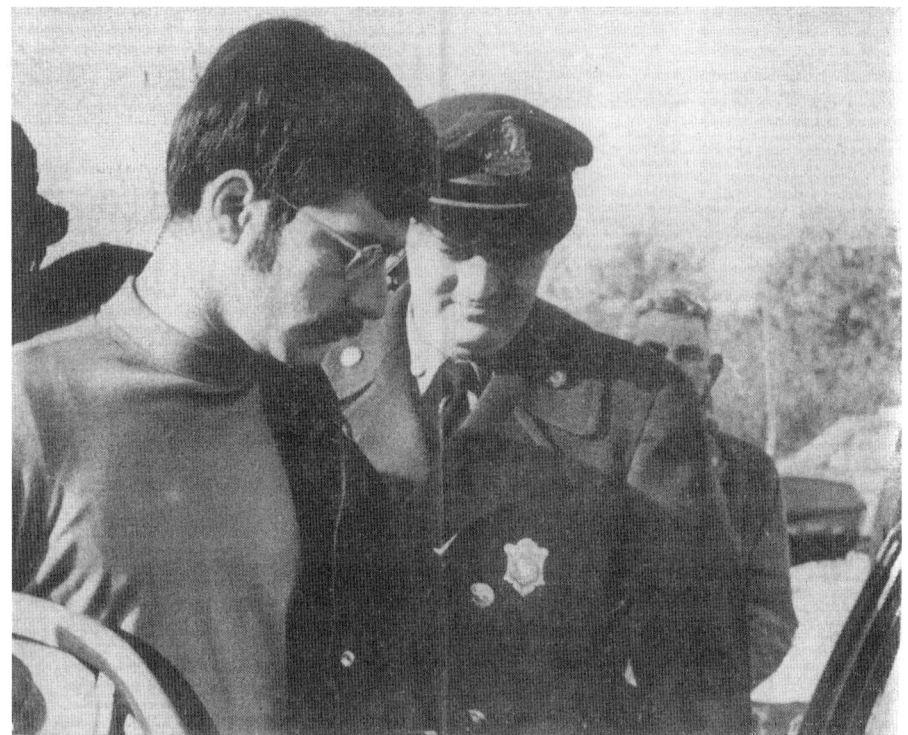

Tony Costa being taken into custody, circa 1969. *Special to the* Cape Cod Standard Times.

head and one in Patricia Walsh's neck. On March 6, 1969, Antone C. Costa, twenty-four, of Provincetown was charged with the murders. He was picked up in a Marlborough Street apartment in Boston and brought to the Provincetown Courthouse in the custody of Lieutenant Detective Bernard Flynn.

Who was Tony Costa and how had he come to commit such heinous crimes? Antone C. Costa was born on August 2, 1944, in Cambridge. A year after he was born, Tony Costa's father drowned after trying to save a shipmate who fell overboard from a destroyer in the Pacific during World War II. In 1946, his mother married Joseph Bonaviri, a stonemason. After the family moved to Cambridge, Massachusetts, Tony's half-brother, Vincent, was born. The family came to Cape Cod after Joseph Bonaviri died. Tony graduated from Provincetown High School in 1962.

On April 20, 1963, Tony married Provincetown teenager Avis Johnson. They had three children. Tony worked odd jobs around Provincetown as a handyman and carpenter and was by trade a taxidermist. The couple divorced on August 6, 1968, after Avis charged Costa with cruel and abusive treatment. Afterward, Avis was awarded custody of the children.

In the aftermath of his arrest for murdering the two Providence women, Costa underwent thirty-five days of psychiatric observation at Bridgewater State Hospital after being arraigned in the Second District Court in Provincetown at the beginning of March. During his arraignment, a plea of innocent was entered on his behalf by Defense Attorney Justin Cavanaugh. Prior to his arrest for the two murders, Costa had been serving a six-month sentence for nonsupport of his wife and children. He was given early release on November 8, 1968, after serving less than two months, when he agreed to assist the Provincetown Police Department in a narcotics investigation.

According to a *Cape Cod Standard Times* article from March 16, 1969, "[S]tatements, by the district attorney and his staff, as well as by the two doctors, have been fraught with images of mutilation, sexual perversion and similar diabolical mischief and have even hinted at occultism." Allegations of drug use permeated the trial. There were also several accounts of Costa having taken an unidentified seventeen-year-old girl to the area where the two graves would later be discovered, saying he wanted to show her his "marijuana patch." He had a bow and arrow with him and the young girl said she felt a sharp sting in her back. Costa told her the shooting was accidental. It was also revealed that Costa would burn his wife with a lit cigarette, causing burns severe enough to require medical attention.

The other two young women's remains were investigated and the women identified as Susan E. Perry, eighteen, of Provincetown, and Lee Monzon, nineteen, of Eastham. Remains of the Monzon girl were dug up when Patricia Walsh and Mary Ann Wysocki's remains were discovered. Susan Perry's grave was located by searchers in the same area on February 18, 1969, although identification was not announced until March 21, 1969.

Costa was held in the Barnstable County House of Corrections for fourteen months prior to his May 1970 trial. Although four bodies were found, Costa would stand trial for the two Rhode Island women, with a possible trial later for the other two. Originally, the trial was to be held in Greenfield due to extensive pretrial publicity, but Costa agreed to have the trial in Barnstable.

Fifteen jurors sat during the eleven-day trial. Throughout the trial, Costa's attorneys, Maurice M. Goldman and Justin G. Cavanaugh, based their defense on the fact that Costa was a longtime drug user. Attorney Edward Dinis successfully prosecuted the case. Evidence was also given by a Boston psychiatrist that Costa may have been a borderline schizophrenic. The jury, led by foreman Russell A. Dodge, deliberated for six and a half hours. Costa was convicted on two charges of first-degree murder and sentenced to life in prison with no chance of parole on May 22, 1970, with his sentence to be served in Massachusetts State Prison in Walpole.

On May 12, 1974, Costa was found hanging by his belt from a cell bar by a prison guard making a routine check. He was twenty-nine years old. It was theorized that he was haunted by the hanging death of another inmate a year before, a prisoner he became friendly with while in prison. He was survived by his ex-wife and three children; his mother had died of a heart attack six months after his imprisonment following the trial. Leo Damore, author of *In His Garden*, recounted the Costa murders. Damore noted that after his death, Tony Costa was buried in an unmarked grave next to his mother, Cecelia Bonaviri, in St. Peter's Cemetery in Provincetown. "It was…exactly where Costa wanted to be—the consummation of the state of grace in death which he had enacted in terrible rituals at a clearing in the woods of Truro."

SUICIDE WATCH

Bridge Leapers

For many years, the Bourne and Sagamore Bridges have been magnets for people desperate to end their lives. In the twenty years before suicide barriers were installed by the Army Corps of Engineers, fifty-four people jumped to their deaths, one hundred threatened suicide and eight people survived a leap. The curved, twelve-foot-high, suicide-prevention barriers installed in 1981 and 1983 have made it difficult, if not impossible, to leap into the 17.4-mile-long Cape Cod Canal, although a few have succeeded. In 1984, a New Bedford man plunged to his death after squeezing through a rare opening caused by powerful winds that blew a tractor-trailer against a section of the barriers.

Many of the jumpers were in their twenties and were often despondent about a job loss or a relationship gone sour, although occasionally there were reports of even younger suicide victims. In September 1974, a sixteen-year-old boy jumped from the Bourne Bridge, and his body wasn't located until three weeks later. Sometimes witnesses reported seeing someone jump, but no body was ever recovered. Often police were alerted to the possibility of a bridge jumper by the presence of abandoned vehicles or, as happened in November 1969, a woman's handbag that was found on the east side of the Sagamore Bridge. Often medical examiners ruled a death caused by jumping from one of the bridges as a "suicide by drowning." Other people have occasionally been arrested for scaling the bridges. A fox even leaped to its death off Bourne Bridge in November 1985. There was speculation that the animal had become disoriented by Route 25 construction and jumped from the bridge.

Police and firefighters from Bourne were often called in for rescue attempts with the Army Corps of Engineers patrol boat sent to locate the jumper. Police were also called in to help subdue people attempting to climb the bridge's suicide fence. The attempted suicides were often as dangerous for the responding police and firefighters as for the jumper. In 1994, a woman flashed a thirteen-inch fishing knife at approaching officers. Fortunately, she dropped the knife during a struggle with police officers and was handcuffed to the fence. She was later removed from the bridge by Bourne firefighters using ropes and pulleys.

The Samaritans, a suicide prevention group founded by Cape Cod resident Monica Dickens, the granddaughter of Charles Dickens, erected signs in 1979 to alert potential suicide victims that there was counseling help available. The goal was to help people consider their actions before they did something drastic.

A forty-one-year-old Wareham man died as recently as 2012, after leaping from the Bourne Bridge. The man was reported to state police after he was seen scaling the bridge fence. His body was later discovered floating in the canal and pulled out around 9:25 a.m. Another suspected suicide prior to this was reported in the *Cape Cod Times* in 2002. This death was particularly distressing since the Samaritans of Cape Cod and the Islands had recently installed new signs at both the Bourne and Sagamore Bridges.

SUICIDE ALLEY

A section of Route 6, the highway that takes visitors from Bourne to Provincetown, also has another name: "Suicide Alley." The stretch from Dennis to Orleans, in particular (Exits 9 to 12), is hazardous because the highway narrows to two single lanes. From 1970 to 1989, thirty-six people were killed in highway accidents on this 12.8-mile stretch, most involving head-on collisions.

The tragedy that thrust "Suicide Alley" into the spotlight was a head-on crash that killed a young mother and her two children. On April 18, 1989, a Brewster woman, Lois Ann Scholomiti, and her children, Lauren and Nicholas, died in Brewster when their eastbound station wagon veered into the oncoming lane and collided head-on with a truck. It was this tragedy that finally set into motion plans to make "Suicide Alley" safer for drivers. The improvements, completed in 1991, included installation of a three-foot-wide berm and reflectors along the center line, road-widening and laws that forbade all passing.

Then, on August 29, 1998, Kathleen "Kay" Bader, retired head librarian at Snow Library in Orleans, died in a crash along this same dangerous ribbon of road. She was between Exits 10 and 11 in East Harwich at the time of the accident. More recently, Angela Champ, a nineteen-year-old Harwich woman, died when her car crossed the center line and collided with a Chrysler minivan on the highway near the Orleans town line. Although the minivan flipped as a result of the accident, the elderly occupants were treated for injuries that weren't considered life-threatening. Efforts continue to make this stretch of highway safe for residents and visitors.

CAPE COD'S MOVIE PAST

Many films have been produced on or about Cape Cod. In recent years, Freddie Prinze Jr. did a stint with the Cape Cod Baseball League in the 2001 movie *Summer Catch*. A 1995 remake of the classic movie *Sabrina*, this one starring Harrison Ford and Julia Ormond, was shot in Chilmark and Vineyard Haven on Martha's Vineyard. However, film directors and producers have been attracted to the Cape and Islands for more than one hundred years.

In 1896, the silent film *Rip Van Winkle* was shot on Cape Cod. It is the earliest surviving motion picture made in New England. Filmed in Buzzards Bay on the estate of New York stage actor Joseph Jefferson, the movie also starred the famous actor. It was shot with an eight-hundred-pound Mutograph camera. According to the Internet Movie Database, the film has a running time of four minutes and was released in May 1903.

The Edison Company filmed *The Landing of the Pilgrims* in Plymouth in 1915. According to the *Cape Cod Times*, the log cabins in which the Pilgrims lived were painted into the background. Miles Standish was played by Duncan McRae, John Alden by Richard Tucker and Priscilla by Margaret Prussing.

Later, in 1917, the Edison Company made *Quaint Provincetown*. According to a 1997 *Cape Cod Times* article, the film "shows the streets of Provincetown as they were 80 years ago. Children are featured playing hide and seek, ships with big masts are seen in the harbor and fishermen are filmed mending nets."

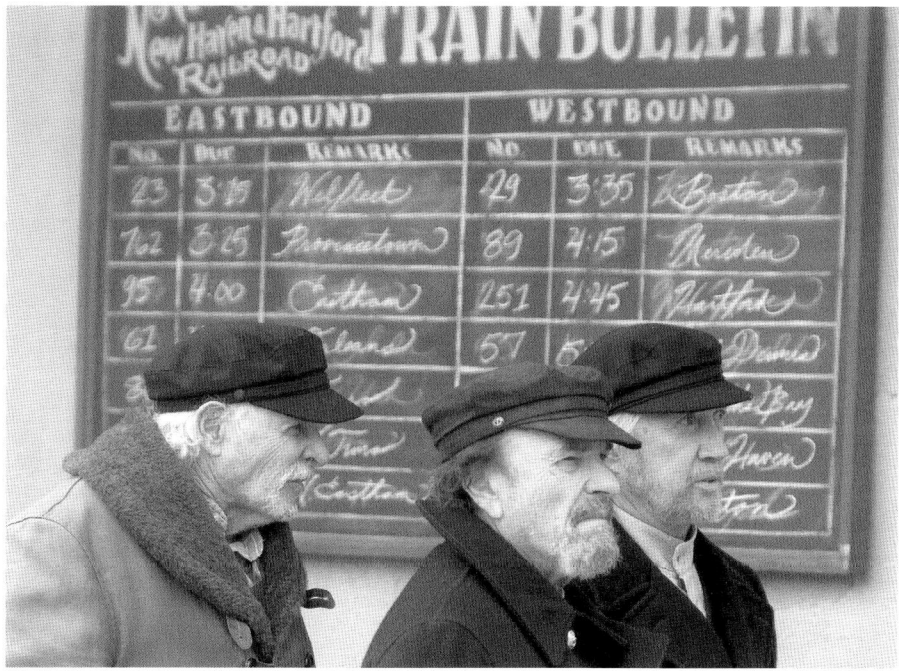

Actors Bruce Dern, Rip Torn and David Carradine portray aging sea captains in the movie *The Golden Boys. Courtesy of the* Cape Cod Times.

Cape Cod has also been featured as a backdrop in several recent motion pictures, including two notable films shot in Chatham. In 2007, the romantic comedy *The Golden Boys*, directed by Daniel Adams, hit local theaters. It starred David Carradine, Rip Torn and Bruce Dern as three seventy-year-old retired sea captains looking for a wife. The idea was that one would marry an attractive middle-aged woman, played by Mariel Hemingway, with the agreement that the other two men could live with the married couple. The film, based on the Joseph Lincoln novel *Cap'n Eri*, was originally called *Chatham*.

In 1952, the U.S. Coast Guard made a daring rescue off Chatham shores after the oil tanker *Pendleton* was destroyed during a blizzard. The 2016 Disney film *The Finest Hours* depicted the daring rescue of men from the *Pendleton*, by a thirty-six-foot Coast Guard motor lifeboat during the height of the storm. The *Cape Cod Times* described the dramatic event: "[F]our young Chatham Coast Guardsmen braved high seas, wind and driving snow in a small wooden CG-36500 to save the 32 seamen that day from the sinking stern section. Seven crewmen and the tanker's captain lost their lives when the bow sank."

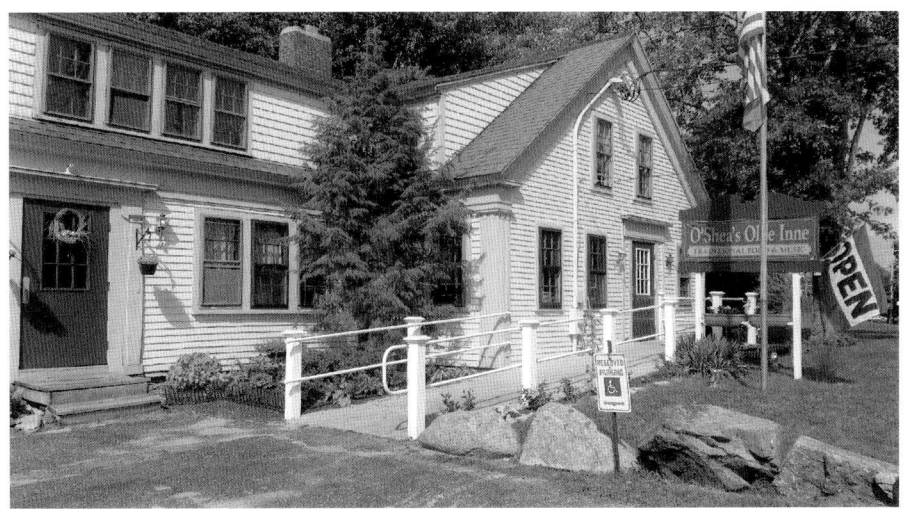

O'Shea's Olde Inne in West Dennis. *Courtesy of Gregory R. Johnson.*

The filmmakers, including Disney producer James Whitaker, wanted the film to be as authentic as possible to the actual rescue. Shooting began in Quincy, Massachusetts, in 2014 at the Quincy Fore River Shipyard and later moved to several South Shore towns. The final scenes were shot in Chatham in December 2014. The crew fought a nor'easter while filming the scenes, which some in the film crew felt brought more realism to the action.

The films *Joe and Joe* (1996) and *Noelle* (2006) were made on location on Cape Cod and were written and produced by David Wall. Both starred local actor and musician Sean Patrick Brennan.

Joe and Joe featured Brennan and actor David Wysocki as two likeable losers who learn about possible treasure hidden near their apartment. The movie, produced for $35,000, became an official selection at the Sundance Film Festival.

It took Wall and Brennan nine years to bankroll their next film. Originally titled *Mrs. Worthington's Party* and later changed to *Noelle*, it told the story of a young priest who arrives to shut down the local parish the week before Christmas and encounters resistance from parishioners. The film was spiced with indoor shots of O'Shea's Olde Inn, a pub in West Dennis on the Cape where Brennan has performed regularly.

Perhaps the most famous film ever shot locally was considered to be the very first Hollywood blockbuster movie. *Jaws* arrived in theaters on June 20, 1975, and became a worldwide megahit. Filmed on location

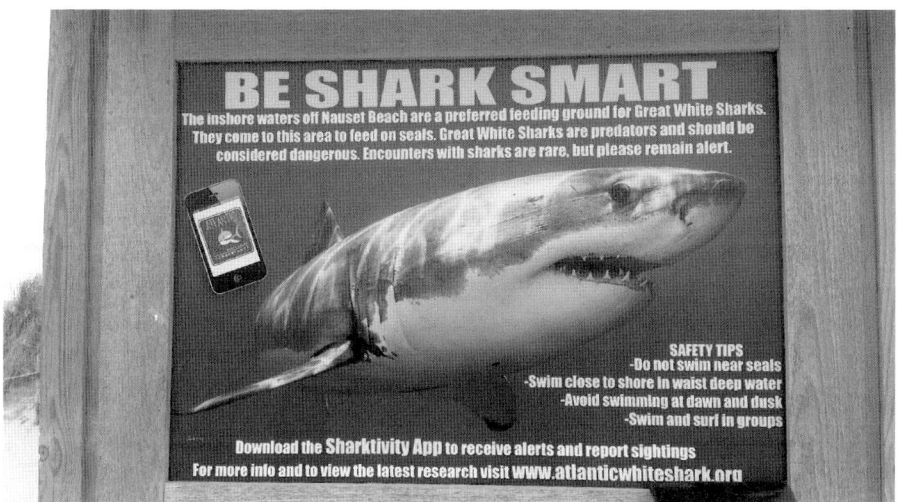

A sign at Nauset Beach in Orleans: "Be Shark Smart." *Courtesy of Cynthia Sherrick Mitchell.*

in Martha's Vineyard, the film starred veteran actors Roy Scheider and Robert Shaw, along with newcomer Richard Dreyfuss. Set in the fictional town, Amity Island, the film was directed by Steven Spielberg and based on the eponymous novel by author Peter Benchley about a town terrorized by a huge shark. Many locals were hired as extras and also contributed props for the production. A 2009 *Cape Cod Times* article noted that Martha's Vineyard was chosen for the film location because "it was the only place on the East Coast that film crews could travel 12 miles out to sea and find a 30-foot sandy bottom that the mechanical shark could work on." The film became hugely successful, winning Academy Awards for best original musical score, film editing and sound mixing and also garnering a nomination for Best Picture. The simple yet terrifying score made its mark for composer John Williams.

A TRIO OF CREATIVE WOMEN

JOSEPHINE DIGNES HURT: PROVINCETOWN ACTRESS

Provincetown has an affinity for actors, or perhaps vice versa. Many famous thespians had their start there, including Eugene O'Neill (an actor as well as a playwright), John (Jack) Reed, Susan Glaspell, Bette Davis and Paul Robeson. Some Provincetown natives discovered a joy for acting and left to pursue their calling elsewhere.

Such was the story of Josephine Dignes Hurt. As a little girl, she first acted at age three, and starred in Christine Foster's dancing school revue between acts on the Wharf Theater. She continued dancing through her school years and studied violin under Albert Nassi. In 1943, she graduated from Provincetown High School. At age eighteen, she even worked for a short time as a *Cape Cod Standard Times* delivery girl in order to buy a special jacket.

She enrolled at Bennington College but only made it through her second semester. During a trip to New York City, she heard about a USO group that was auditioning talent for *Oklahoma!* She was accepted into the group and spent the end of World War II playing to soldiers in New Guinea and the Philippines. The *Cape Cod Standard Times* in December 1945 noted that "they played to 1,700,000 soldiers and sailors in the Southwest Pacific and, in addition, gave 50 special performances in front line hospitals, evacuation hospitals and base hospitals." At times, these performances came under enemy bombing raids. She met her husband, Fred Hurt, in Manila, where he was serving. When Fred visited her for four days, the young couple discovered there were no rooms available, but a general with a romantic heart gave up his room at the hotel so they could be together.

After the war, Hurt got her first big role starring as the leading lady in *Brigadoon* at the Ziegfeld Theater in New York City. She later recorded the song "Zip" from *Pal Joey* and had a part in *Cradle Will Rock*, in which she was cast as the daughter of the star, Shirley Booth. With television in its infancy, Jo decided to try her hand at the new medium. For a year, she sang and yodeled as Josie Bell Shufflebottom in the CBS show *Corn Cobblers*. Among her many television appearances were roles in *The Member of the Wedding* and *The Star Wagon* with a young Dustin Hoffman. In 1958, she returned to her roots by playing in *Most Happy Fella* at the Melody Tent in Hyannis. She came back again in 1964 to appear in the Richard Rodgers production of *No Strings*. She said herself that she never lost her love for Cape Cod. The Provincetown/New York stage connection continues to the present day. For this young starstruck actress, it meant a wonderful life.

LA MERI (RUSSELL MERIWETHER HUGHES)

One truly amazing transplant to Cape Cod was the ethnic dancer Russell Meriwether Hughes, known professionally as "La Meri." She founded Ethnic Dance Arts Inc. in 1970 with hopes of building a performing arts center off Route 132 near Cape Cod Community College in West Barnstable. She moved to Cape Cod in 1957 for what she called her "first retirement," but she was anything but retiring.

The talented performer was born in Louisville, Kentucky, and later moved to San Antonio in 1910. As a child, she studied ballet and Spanish and Mexican dance. Her passion for ethnic dance would guide her life. She made her stage debut in 1924 at the Rialto Theater, where she danced prologues to silent movies. Early in her career, she changed her name because she felt her given name was too masculine. During the 1920s and '30s, she toured the world and became interested in the dances of India and Spain. In 1940, she founded the School of Natya in New York with Ruth St. Denis. Here, she taught classes and performed with her company, the Five Natyas. Around this time, dance critic John Martin wrote in the *New York*

Times that "an afternoon with Miss La Meri is rather like being shown a small corner of some connoisseur's collection of choreographiana."

When she traveled, La Meri tried to stay at one location as long as she could to learn the local dances. She looked for the most typical of the dances of a country and also purchased costumes to accompany the performances. She loved Indian dances and music. In an interview with Alice Horn of the *New Bedford Standard Times*, she was quoted as saying that she couldn't dance in toe rings because wearing ballet shoes closed the spaces between her toes. She also said that the difference between western and eastern dancing was that "in the East you start from the top, in the West from the feet."

She was a Renaissance woman who taught at universities and wrote six volumes of poetry and five books on

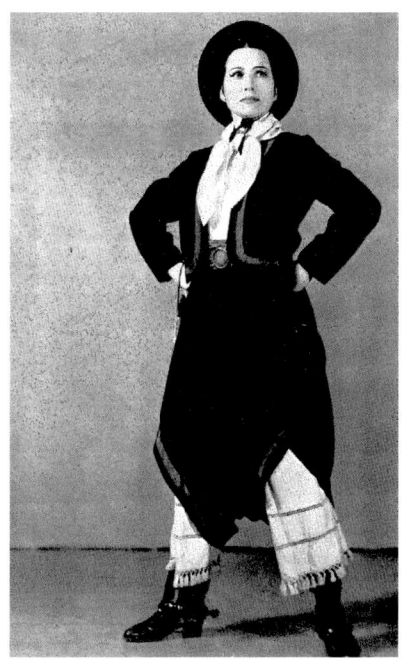

Photo of ethnic dancer La Meri (Russell Meriwether Hughes), circa 1944. *Courtesy of the* Cape Cod Times.

dance. A 1968 *Cape Cod Standard Times* article described her as "the dance enchantress of a thousand and one nights. Her tales are of comedy, romance, epic deed and native folklore, and her stage is the world and the entire world her audience." La Meri visited Cape Cod while under contract to the Cape Cod Conservatory of Music and fell in love with the area.

Once she moved to Hyannis, La Meri taught classes in the basement of her home and held classes in dance three nights a week at the Barnstable Comedy Club theater. She also hosted yearly festivals of ethnic dance. She introduced her extensive costume collection as well as music from around the world. In 1972, she received the prestigious Capezio Dance Award. In 1984, she took her "second retirement" and moved to San Antonio, where she died on January 7, 1988, at age eighty-nine. Her greatest dream, a local world-class performing arts center, didn't materialize, but her vision and passion for dance left an indelible mark on the arts of Cape Cod.

DOROTHY LAKE GREGORY: A PROVINCETOWN TREASURE

In the early years of my marriage, I heard many tales of my husband's childhood summer vacations in Provincetown, where he and his sister visited their grandparents Ross Moffett and Dorothy Lake Gregory, famed Provincetown artists. As a little boy, he delighted in wandering the streets and byways, playing on the sandy beaches and going with his grandmother to buy Portuguese bread in the bakery across the street. He remembers his grandfather as a quiet man who spent countless hours painting in his studio. By contrast, his grandmother was tiny and outgoing. Everyone who passed them on Commercial Street knew her.

Gradually, I learned more about Greg's grandmother. She was born in Brooklyn, New York, in 1893 and showed interest in art from an early age. Her father was Grant Gregory, one-time night editor at the *New York Tribune*. By the time she was eight, Dorothy was making pen-and-ink sketches of children on roller skates for the newspapers. She received some art training

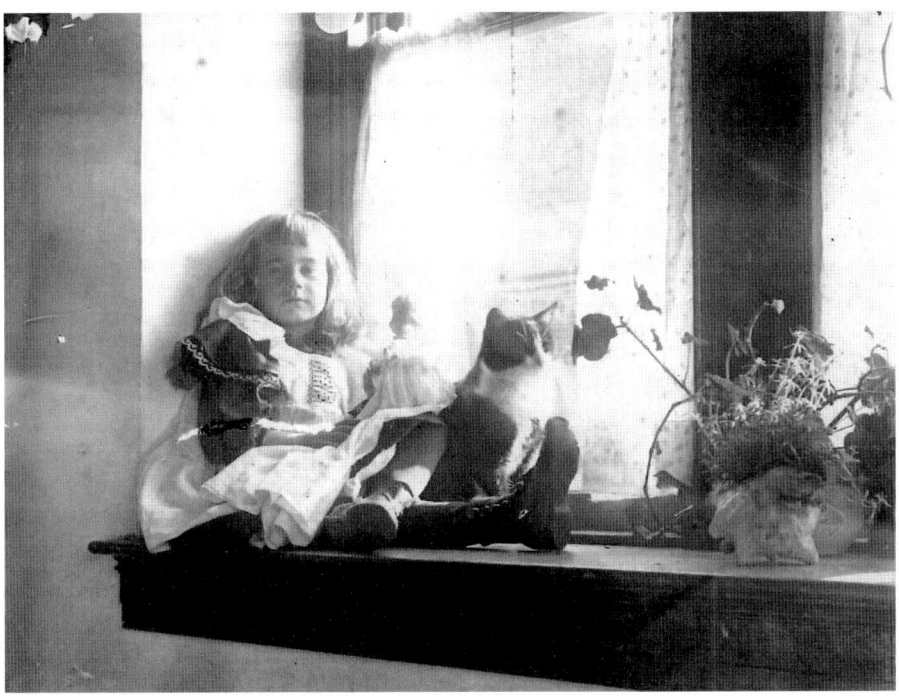

A young Dorothy Lake Gregory sits in a window seat with her cat. *From the estate of Alan W. Moffett.*

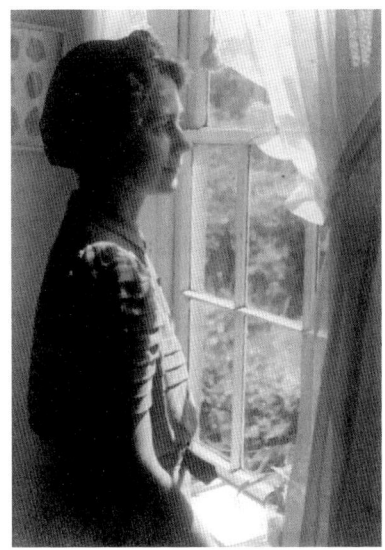

Dorothy Lake Gregory around the time of her marriage, circa 1920. *From the estate of Alan W. Moffett.*

in Brooklyn public schools. Later, at age sixteen, she studied in Paris at the Julian Academy. One of her favorite pastimes was to visit the Louvre, where she could study the old masters. When she returned home, she enrolled first at the Pratt Institute in New York and later won a scholarship to the Arts Students League and studied with Robert Henri. It was here that she met her future husband, Ross Moffett. At the urging of a fellow student, she moved to Provincetown in 1914 to study with Charles Hawthorne.

She and Moffett reconnected in Provincetown, where Moffett had moved in 1913. They married and remained together for nearly fifty-one years. In her biography of Ross Moffett, *Figures in a Landscape*, author Josephine wrote about their early years together. "Upon leaving their rooming house at first light, they would go directly to the Portuguese bakery to buy a loaf of fresh bread and then head off to the studio where they breakfasted on Portuguese bread toasted on top of an old wood laundry stove. After this simple 'La Boheme' repast, Ross painted and Dorothy drew."

At this time in her young marriage, Dorothy began doing newspaper and book illustrations. In fact, the *New York Times* once ran a whole column of her drawings on the front page. She later became interested in doing lithographs after her brother, photographer John Gregory, bought an eight-hundred-pound lithographic press. One of her best-known prints is "Alice and the White Knight." She was dissatisfied with the John Tenniel illustrations in the classic *Alice in Wonderland* and *Through the Looking Glass*, so she decided to do her own. She also did a series of paintings for the Andrew Lang fairy tale series. Her *Green Fairy Tale* book sits on my bookshelf at home.

During her lifetime, Dorothy exhibited at the Metropolitan Museum of Art, the Brooklyn Museum and the Art Institute of Cape Cod, among others. She also illustrated more than twenty books and magazines. The Smithsonian Archives of American Art is the repository for the Ross and Dorothy Lake Gregory Moffett papers, circa 1870–1992. According to the Smithsonian website, the papers of Dorothy Moffett "include family letters, photographs, a journal and original artwork providing scattered documentation of her life and career as a printmaker and illustrator." She died in 1975 and is buried along with her husband, son and daughter in Provincetown Cemetery. According to a 1947 *Cape Cod Standard Times* article, her drawings and paintings depicted "how children would imagine dwarfs, rabbits, roosters and all the heroes and villains of a child's world."

MAIL DELIVERY

PAST AND PRESENT

Old-Fashioned Mail Delivery

The first record of any official mail deliveries on Cape Cod was that of mail carrier John Smith. In 1654, he was paid by the governor of Plymouth County to carry letters between that settlement and Nauset. Interestingly, there is no record of whether he was on horseback or using horse and buggy. In the early American colonies, there was no organized postal service until the late seventeenth century, and even then, it operated much differently than it does today. Before this time, the Americans relied on friends, merchants and sometimes even the Native American population to deliver their mail for them.

In 1775, regular postal service was set up between Cambridge, Plymouth, Sandwich and Falmouth on a once-a-week basis. Then, in 1790, Cape Cod's own "pony express" operation started running between Plymouth and Sandwich, with the depot at Fessenden Tavern on the site of what is today's Dan'l Webster Inn. The tavern was a former parsonage occupied by the Reverend Benjamin Fessenden, whose son, Thomas, converted the house into a tavern after his father's death.

With interest in building faster and more efficient mail service, post horseback riders began delivering U.S. mail between Boston and Barnstable in 1792. The mailman would set off from Barnstable on a Tuesday morning and spend the night in Plymouth. The following night, he delivered the mail to the Boston postmaster at the Sign of the Lion on Washington Street. He would then leave Thursday morning and complete his trip the following night. For his trouble, the rider would make a dollar a day, considered good pay at the time.

Travel by stagecoach disappeared in the mid-1800s with the advent of railroad travel. Rail service from the mainland extended into Sandwich in 1848, when the stagecoach from Plymouth was dropped. The stagecoach continued to provide transportation to and from Sandwich, New Bedford, Falmouth and towns on the Lower Cape for a few more years before being discontinued.

Nowadays, we can travel by car to Boston in about two hours, not the two days needed by mail riders two hundred years ago.

POST OFFICES ON CAPE COD

A clip from the *Cape Cod Standard Times* dated April 21, 1940, depicts the growth of post offices in the United States and on Cape Cod. According to the article, there were only seventy-five post offices in the United States in 1780; this number had mushroomed to 8,450 post offices by 1830. In that same year, there were 420 post offices in Massachusetts and 38 on Cape Cod. Many of the postmasters listed for 1830 mentioned time-honored Cape Cod surnames. Mathew Cobb was postmaster of Barnstable, while Rowland T. Crocker manned the postal helm in Cotuit and Ebenezer Nye worked in North Falmouth. Other local names included Mayo, Stone, Higgins, Scudder, Hinckley, Perry, Nickerson, Paine, Bangs, Dillingham, Chase, Burgess and Thatcher. The first post office in Centerville was established in 1834, when the town's name was changed from Chequatuet to Centreville.

According to an article on the history of the U.S. post offices, envelopes weren't used in the early part of the nineteenth century. A letter was simply folded and the address placed on the outside of the letter. The customer had to mail and pick up letters at the post office. There was no home delivery except in some large cities. Stamps became available in 1847 but weren't always used. Until 1855, people sent their letters with recipients paying the cost of the mailing. If the letters were refused, the post office lost out on delivery costs. Street boxes for mail collection began to appear by 1858.

Several Cape post offices have colorful histories. The Bourne Post Office was part of the Blackington house near the wooden bridge of the Monument

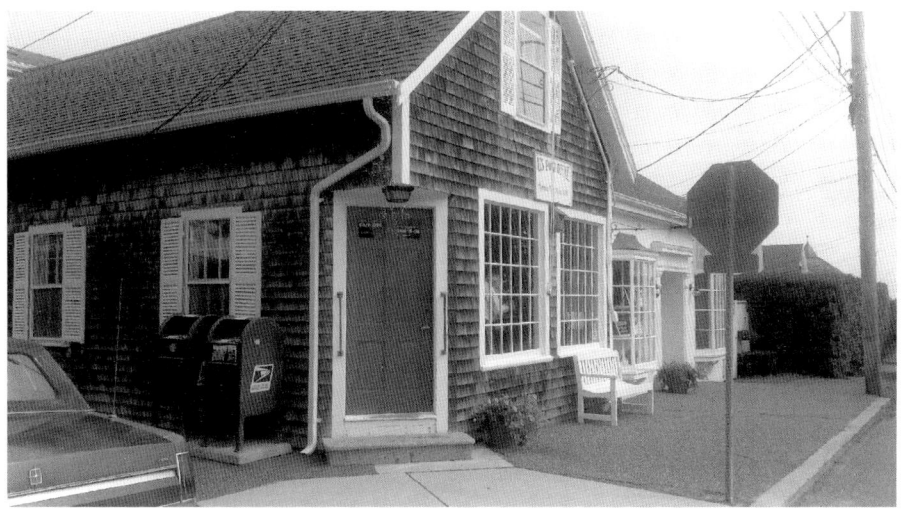

The Hyannis Port Post Office. *Courtesy of Gregory R. Johnson.*

River. It was moved to its present location around 1913, when the canal was being built and its postmaster was Ordello Swift. The tiny Hyannis Port Post Office gained prominence when John F. Kennedy became president in 1961. It was well known for its distinctive red painted door.

The Provincetown Post Office gained notoriety when the entire staff was arrested in 1978 and charged with embezzlement and fraud. This was the first time in U.S. history that the entire staff of a post office was arrested.

Now many Cape post offices have been renovated, expanded or moved due to the need for more space. For the most part, many still have the charm of their old-fashioned predecessors. During the 1930s and 1940s, works of art were funded for post offices by the New Deal. One lovely example is *The Recapture of Corn Schooner from the British* by Karl Oberteuffer (1943), on display at the Falmouth Post Office.

EDGAR ROWE SNOW

HISTORIAN AND "FLYING SANTA"

The author of at least ninety-five books on the lore and history of seafaring New England, Edward Rowe Snow was born in Winthrop, Massachusetts, on August 22, 1902. After graduating from Harvard and Boston universities, he became a high school teacher in Winthrop. During World War II, he served with the XII Bomber Command. Upon his return to the States, he became a daily columnist for the *Patriot Ledger* newspaper in Quincy, Massachusetts, from 1957 to 1982.

It was while he was studying at Boston University that his master's thesis became the basis for his first book, *The Islands of Boston Harbor*. He later described his love for writing about "pirates, treasure, lighthouses, shipwrecks and ghosts." In fact, Snow was an able seaman himself and loved to canoe and sail the New England coastline since he was a boy. He was also athletic and won dozens of medals in track and swimming when he was young.

During his later years as a notable lecturer, Snow would bring along relics, or what he called his "traveling museum," to share with his listeners. These items from famous shipwrecks included a book bound in human skin, a pair of baby shoes, a wooden leg and other fascinating items. During his career, Snow spoke at the Eastham and Falmouth Historical Societies, the Cape Playhouse and at the Olde Colonial Courthouse in Barnstable, with Tales of Cape Cod as his sponsor. He also shot 16mm movies of his trips for use at his various talks and lectures.

Interestingly, although Barry Clifford staked a claim to the treasures from the pirate ship *Whydah* in 1984, Snow attempted to salvage items from the shipwreck as early as 1947 after spotting the wreckage site from a plane. The

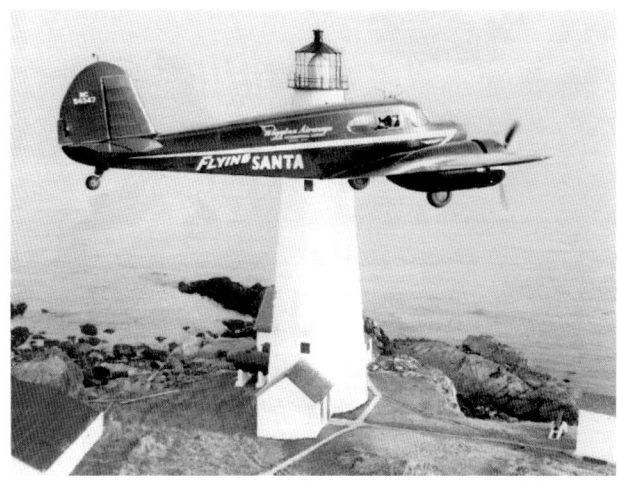

Photo of the "Flying Santa" in front of a lighthouse. *Courtesy of the* Cape Cod Times.

ship wrecked off the Outer Cape in 1717, and its treasures are estimated at $400 million. In September 1947, Snow and his crew attempted to remove an old cannon from the wreck with the help of professional diver Jack Poole. Rough ocean waters thwarted the rescue attempts, and their diving platform was destroyed. He was able to find traces of gold from a chunk torn from the ship's bow that was later taken to Boston for analysis. A *Cape Cod Standard Times* article from 1948 mentioned that Snow had displayed coins from the *Whydah* and a key from a stateroom door from the wreck of the steamer *Portland* (another famous Cape wreck) during an illustrated talk at the Orleans High School.

As well as being a storyteller, Snow became well known around the Cape as the "Flying Santa" who delivered Christmas presents to lighthouse keepers and their families. These annual trips began in 1936, and he was often accompanied by his wife and his daughter, Dorothy. Among the items he delivered every Christmas were candy, gum, children's books, balloons, lollipops, dolls, cigarettes, razors and the latest copy of his newest book. In December 1969 (according to the *Cape Cod Standard Times*), "Snow plans to drop 112 packages to 54 lighthouses and Coast Guard stations between West Quoddy Head, Maine, and Montauk Point, New York." Sometimes the packages he dropped didn't find their intended targets. One time, a package dropped at Portsmouth, New Hampshire, was picked up by a whale expert on Cape Cod, and another package dropped at Eastern Point Light wasn't found for nineteen months. The last year he played "Santa" was in 1980. He died on April 10, 1982. Many of his books are still in print and are enjoyed by a new generation of readers.

CAPE COD ORIGINALS

EDWARD GOREY

One of Cape Cod's most beloved and also most eccentric residents was artist and writer Edward Gorey. He was born in 1925 in Chicago, and after growing up and graduating from Harvard in 1950, he began illustrating book covers for Doubleday. Although he was trying to jumpstart his writing career, he couldn't finish the novels he started, so he began to create smaller books. These were tales of dark humor and whimsy with such titles as *The Gashlycrumb Tinies*, *The Beastly Baby*, *The Doubtful Guest* and the *Dancing Cats and Neglected Murderesses*. In all, he wrote ninety books and illustrated sixty others. He also designed sets and costumes for theater productions. In 1978, he won a Tony Award for costume design for the Broadway production of *Dracula*. He may be most famous for creating the opening and closing titles of the PBS television series *Mystery!*

After living in New York City, Gorey eventually found his place on the Cape—the Elephant House, now the Edward Gorey House, on Strawberry Lane in Yarmouth Port. He lived there until his death in 2000. While he lived on the Cape, Gorey was instrumental in staging many of his stories in theaters around the Cape. For example, Woods Hole actors had fun performing his *Lost Shoelaces* in 1987 at the Woods Hole Community Hall. The play was based on a collection of twenty Gorey short stories. Later, his play *Useful Urns* appeared at the Provincetown Inn in 1990. His *Stumbling*

Christmas was shown at the Theater on the Bay in Buzzards Bay in November 1995. There was an opera for puppets, *The White Canoe*, staged by the Cotuit Center for the Arts. It was Gorey's final theatrical piece.

In an interview with Phil Thomas of the Associated Press in 1984, Gorey described himself as a writer first. "First a writer, then an artist. The drawings come from the writing. After I get an idea for a book, I will sit down and write out my text. Then, I will do the drawings needed to illustrate the text. I have to do it that way, because if I don't the book doesn't work out." In his book *Amphigorey Also*, he wrote about a "loathsome couple." He said he got the idea from reading about a man and woman who murdered children. He went on to say, "I find that the older I get, the fonder I get of those strange little paragraphs that newspapers, especially in England, use to fill up a column on a page." Gorey, of the bearded face, intense gaze and voluminous fur coat, loved the absurd and the whimsical, along with cats, bats and the ballet. A multifaceted man of many talents, Gorey was a master of the art of the macabre.

BENJAMIN SPOCK: "BABY DOCTOR" AND LOCAL ACTIVIST

Dr. Benjamin Spock had a long, honored career as a pediatrician and advisor to thousands of new parents. His classic book, *Baby and Child Care*, is still a bestseller. He believed in following the cues of the infants themselves and advocated feeding on demand and picking up crying babies. His liberal approach was welcome to new mothers who often didn't trust their own instincts.

Dr. Spock was also a longtime Falmouth summer resident and an antiwar activist during the 1960s. In June 1968, Spock, along with three others, was charged with conspiring to counsel young men on avoiding the Vietnam draft. Spock held a press conference after his indictment at which he said, "If going to jail helps the movement, I'm for it. If the government is trying to intimidate us, they will find themselves sadly wrong." He went on to call the draft resisters courageous, patriotic young men.

A twelve-man U.S. District Court jury found him guilty on charges to "counsel, aid and abet young men to evade the draft." He was sentenced to two years in prison but didn't serve out his term. Before the verdict, Judge Francis J.W. Ford Jr. instructed the jury, "There's no freedom to violate the laws of the United States because one believes the law is illegal or unconstitutional." Spock was allowed to remain free on bail while his case was appealed, with the charges ultimately being dismissed.

Born on May 2, 1903, in New Haven, Connecticut, Spock attended Phillips Academy and Yale University. While at Yale, he studied history and literature and later was a member of the Olympic rowing team that won a gold medal at the 1924 Paris Olympics. He graduated from Columbia University's College of Physicians and Surgeons in 1929. His now famous book was published in 1946 and has sold more than 50 million copies in forty-nine languages.

In a 1966 *Cape Cod Standard Times* article, Spock scolded parents for allowing junior high school–age children to play kissing games or have dates. Described as a "Falmouth colonist," Spock also reprimanded fathers for being overly involved in Little League activities. He went on to address the problem of "teeny weenies" or the "pre-bra set" whose parents "for their own enjoyment, invite a young child to mimic an adult shouting about love." He warned that this might cause the child to cheapen love and impair his or her idealism.

It's unclear how long the famous physician summered in Falmouth. In his later years, he lived aboard his boats and sailed in Maine in the summers. He died on March 15, 1998, at age ninety-four, at his home in La Jolla, California, of respiratory failure. He was praised by Cape pediatricians for being the doctor who sought to "teach us to understand and listen to children."

A Salute to Nantucket's "Madaket Millie"

On March 24, 1990, a contingent of Coast Guardsmen, along with friends and even beloved dogs, saluted Nantucket's "Madaket Millie." They were there to say goodbye to a woman who had watched over Madaket Harbor for more than fifty years. The village of Madaket is situated in the western end of Nantucket.

Mildred Jewitt was born in 1907 and performed her first maritime rescue at age eleven. She continued her role of "seaside sentinel" throughout her life. During World War II, she patrolled the beaches in the area and trained German shepherd dogs for patrol duty in all branches of the military. She is also remembered as the first person to discover the Panamanian freighter

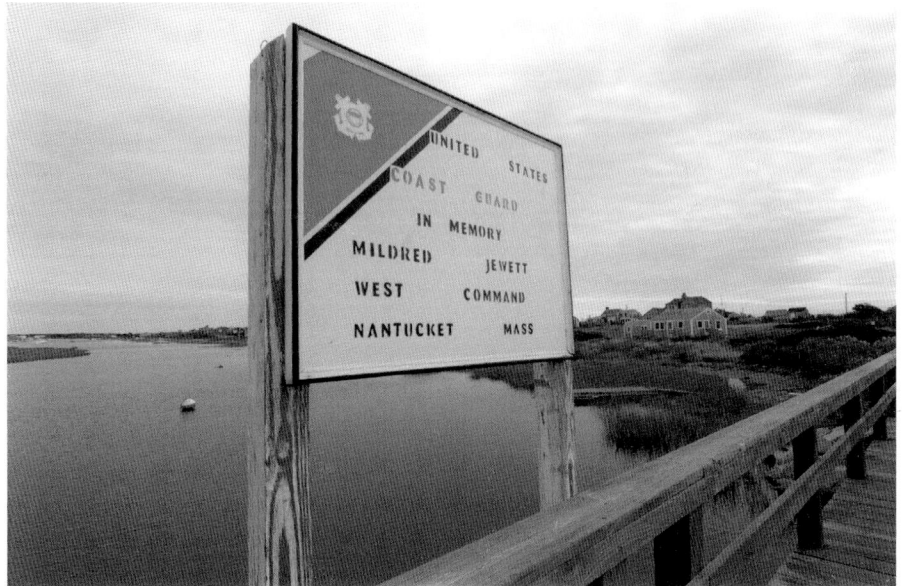

A Coast Guard sign dedicated to the memory of Mildred "Madaket Millie" Jewitt. *Courtesy of the* Cape Cod Times.

Kotor that was stranded on the beach the same day the Madaket Coast Guard station closed in 1947. Coast Guard officials gave her much of the credit for freeing the vessel in a timely manner from low water within a day.

According to local lore, Millie once killed a 300-pound sand shark with a pitchfork and, on another occasion, hoisted and carried a 283-pound log from the beach. She was described in one 1980 *Cape Cod Times* article as a "rugged old bird, but a nice lady."

Her great love was the Coast Guard, and she held the honorary rank of chief warrant officer 4 (bosun). In 1985, she was promoted to chief warrant officer twenty years after receiving her honorary rank. After her "piping" ceremony, the officiating admiral asked if she had anything to say. "It's about time," she responded.

Known as a crusty individual, she hated having her photo taken and once tried to push a *Cape Cod Times* reporter off a pier when he tried to take her picture. Kind and curt by turns, "Madaket Millie" loved animals of all kinds, but especially dogs. She lived a long life, with duty first to her "family," the Coast Guard. The sign on her house read, "Coast Guard West End Command," and she displayed weather warnings on her flagpole for mariners.

"Madaket Millie" died at age eighty-seven and is remembered as a unique figure in local Nantucket island lore. At her memorial service, Coast Guard chaplain Commodore Thomas Chatwick suggested that the best way to remember her was to "look out at the coastline Millie held so important in her life." A flag and photographs were donated to the Nantucket Lifesaving Museum to help keep her memory alive.

THE UNIQUE PHOTOGRAPHY OF SAMUEL CHAMBERLAIN

A chronicler of Cape Cod landscapes, photographer Samuel Chamberlain published his book, *Cape Cod in the Sun*, in 1937. It is filled with evocative black-and-white photos of Cape Cod at the beginning of the twentieth century. In the foreword is written: "There is nothing quite like Cape Cod in these broad United States. This audacious hook of sandy soil, projecting far into the Atlantic, leaves an unforgettable impression upon all who pay it a visit. Its charm is subtle and hard to define. It has remained its own leisurely self, an example of calm, simple, dignified living. Upon it the haste and vulgarity of the outside world have barely left an imprint. It hasn't got a skyscraper or a street car or a bread line."

Chamberlain's photos take the reader across Cape Cod, starting with a spectacular photo of the Cape Cod Canal and touching on each Cape town in turn. Most of his photos are of landscapes, portraying scenes of barren seascapes with a single lonely tree or historic homes where shadows stretch across wide lawns. There are also photographs of windmills, harbors, churches, icehouses and fields with old stone walls. The cover photo features Chamberlain's photo "The Village Street, Yarmouth Port." The photo is framed by a goose-lined archway with a pump beneath. In the distance, an antique car (well, at least to us) is parked by a white building with black shutters. A dirt road (now Route 6A) meanders into the distance. It captures some of Cape Cod's mystery and quiet solitude.

In the middle of the book is a centerfold of Cape doorways from Falmouth to Yarmouth Port to Wellfleet. Some are welcoming, while others seem shuttered and shadowed. One unique photograph shows a dead tree with long branches reaching into a dark sky. Beyond the tree is a barn with a rutted path winding through short grasses. The compositions are striking and lonely. There are also photos of beaches, dunes, inlets, boats and pine forests. In another photo, a North Truro lighthouse dominates the foreground. Figures of people line the lookout post but seem part of the architecture itself. In the caption, Chamberlain wrote, "From this trim white tower flashes one of the most powerful lights in the world." The photos are reminiscent of another famous Cape photographer, John Gregory, with their emphasis on light and shadow.

Fast-forward to the summer of 2008. The Cahoon Museum of American Art in Cotuit presented a retrospective of Samuel Chamberlain's works. The exhibit was titled "The Past and Present: Vintage Photographs of Samuel Chamberlain." The photos in the exhibit were from Chamberlain's original negatives, housed at the Boston Public Library and Phillips Library at Peabody-Essex Museum, which also holds all of his papers. He came to Cape Cod in 1936 and later returned in 1953, when he created *Cape Cod: A Photographic Sketchbook.*

The stark beauty of the photos that lined the walls of several rooms in the downstairs portion of the museum captivated the viewer. There were also sketchbooks and letters from Chamberlain to his wife and publisher. As the caption on the cover of the *Cape Cod Times* weekly arts and entertainment section, "CapeWeek," read at the time of the exhibit, "Photography exhibit frames Cape's place in history." Samuel Chamberlain died on January 11, 1975, in Marblehead, Massachusetts. He was also distinguished for his work as a printmaker, artist and writer but is best remembered by Cape Codders for his photographs that captured Cape Cod just prior to the Second World War.

KEEPING A CAPE WEATHER EYE

Weather has always been a topic of discussion on Cape Cod. From nor'easters to hurricanes, blizzards and dense fog, the locals enjoy the ever-changing seasons and the ensuing inclement weather. As Mark Twain reportedly said, "If you don't like the weather in New England, just wait a few minutes."

Charles F. Sleeper of Hyannis began keeping official weather forecasts on January 1, 1892, and continued through February 1, 1915. George H. Palmer held the post of local weatherman from May 15, 1916, through February 1930. During this time, Cape Cod saw several destructive weather systems. In August 1904, an extratropical storm with hurricane-force winds roared across southern New England, doing damage in Martha's Vineyard and Buzzards Bay. On July 21, 1916, a Category 1 hurricane with wind speeds of eighty-five miles per hour crossed Cape Cod. A year later, in August 1917, a tropical storm sank four ships passing offshore of Nantucket, killing forty-one sailors. In August 1924, another Category 1 hurricane moved over Cape Cod causing widespread damage, including downed trees and structural damage.

Beginning in March 1930, the State Normal School in Hyannis served as the official weather post through January 1945. The most damaging storm in this period was the New England Hurricane of 1938, during which wind gusts of Category 5 strength passed over eastern Connecticut, Rhode Island and southern New England. The storm killed more than six hundred people and is considered the worst storm in the area up to the present.

Warren Sperl began his stint as weather observer on May 1, 1946, and continued through March 1953. Shortly after he stepped down, Cape Cod bore the brunt of Hurricane Carol on August 31, 1954, which made landfall as a Category 3 hurricane. Extreme damage was reported in southern New England. This storm is also remembered because a sister storm, Hurricane Edna, came ashore only two weeks later on September 11, 1954. Winds reached 125 miles per hour in Chilmark on Martha's Vineyard.

After March 17, 1963, observations were made at the Cape & Vineyard Electric Company. Weather was also monitored by the U.S. Coast Guard Lighthouse keeper in Chatham from March 1898 to December 1952, when the observatory was moved to the Race Point Lighthouse Station in Provincetown. Other notable storms in recent years include Hurricane Gloria on September 27, 1985, and the last hurricane to make a direct hit on Cape Cod was Hurricane Bob, on August 19, 1991. Cape Cod also felt the effects of Hurricane Irene in 2011 and Superstorm Sandy in 2012. For the people who lived through these historic storms, the memory of intense winds, storm surge, downed trees and power lines will remain for years to come.

Winter Fires: Hot Times in Cold Weather

Somehow the idea of fires spreading in any geographic area makes one think of late summer or early fall, when the temperatures are hot and steamy. The truth, however, is that fires happen year-round. The Cape hasn't been immune to fires over the past one hundred years.

On January 24, 1896, the Hyannis State Normal School on Main Street was destroyed by fire fifteen days after opening. In 1904, a "Hyannis conflagration" destroyed fifteen buildings on Main Street. In 1943, the Colonial building on Main Street in Hyannis burned down and took the life of a Maritime cadet. Another memorable local fire happened on February 3, 1959, when the Hyannis Clothing Center was destroyed by flames. The fire damages were estimated at $100,000. It was by far the worst fire in sixteen years, according to news reports of the time.

One more recent winter fire happened on January 4, 2003, when a homeless man was rescued from a burning warehouse on Route 132. Firefighters had to cut through welded doors to gain access, and the man was rescued via a thermal imaging camera. According to the Hyannis

Fire Department, the former Old Harbor Cracker Barrel factory was also heavily damaged in a fire that occurred during a heavy snowstorm in November 2005.

The U.S. Fire Administration lists cooking as the leading cause of winter fires. More than nine hundred people die in winter home fires every year. The threat of winter fires is real, and Cape Codders have shown courage and resourcefulness in battling such blazes at any time of year.

LONG-AGO NOR'EASTER

As a child growing up on Cape Cod, I remember many storms. The most feared were the nor'easters that hit mostly during the winter months. At the time of one memorable nor'easter that occurred in my early childhood, our family home in Orleans was situated across from a marsh, so there weren't many trees to break the path of a strong wind.

Of course, this was long before the Weather Channel and easy access to news. My dad always loved to tease us with "a great day for the ducks" when rain threatened. A sunny day, by contrast, was "a great day for the race" (as in the human race). So, we had to rely on our senses to know when bad weather was brewing. Many houses at that time had weather vanes that whirled and spun during very windy days.

The nor'easter hit when I was nine or ten years old. My sisters and I spent the better part of three days inside our house, listening to the keening of the winds outside. Rain pelted the house, and the skies never lightened. My mother made our time enjoyable by bringing out a card table where we played games, did puzzles and made Christmas ornaments. She lit a kerosene lamp to help us see since the power had gone out.

It was cozy to be with family but also lonely. We were so isolated in that house so near the sea. As the storm intensified, it seemed like giants were unleashed. In Theodore Roethke's poem "The Storm," he writes, "A fine fume of rain driving in from the sea,/Riddling the sand, like a wide spray of buckshot,/The wind from the sea and the wind from the mountain contending,/Flicking the foam from the whitecaps straight upward into the darkness." In my child's mind, the storm was fierce and impersonal.

The list of local storms I have experienced could fill a small volume: Hurricane Gloria, Hurricane Bob, Tropical Storm Bertha, the Perfect

Storm, the remnants of Hurricane Noel, the near misses of Hurricane Edouard and Earl and the Blizzard of '05. Although I'm not sure what year it came to our shores, the storm I remember is a nor'easter that blew through my girlhood dreams, a no-name storm of epic proportions. I am reminded of this early experience in every storm that has followed.

PRESIDENTIAL VISITS

Cape Cod and the Islands have served as a magnet for visitors, day trippers and summer renters for many years, but also for U.S. presidents. Many have come for the salty air, clean beaches, lively art scene and golfing opportunities. It all started with President Grover Cleveland.

GRAY GABLES:
GROVER CLEVELAND'S SUMMER RETREAT

Before John F. Kennedy spent summers in Hyannis Port, before Bill Clinton and Barack Obama visited Martha's Vineyard, Grover Cleveland called Bourne his summer home. He settled his young family in a large summer "cottage" in an area now known as Gray Gables. His friend, the famous actor Joseph Jefferson, had recommended Bourne as a good spot for a summer retreat. Cleveland was interested in trout fishing, and the lure of trout-filled ponds induced him to purchase his summer home around 1891. The place was originally built in 1880 by Frederick Tudor Jr. and called Tudor Haven. Cleveland changed the name to match the home's weathered shingles and numerous gables. He even had a private railroad station built.

Before he became president, Cleveland was the governor of New York. He was the first Democrat elected after the Civil War. When he married twenty-one-year-old Frances Folsom in 1886 at the White House, his new

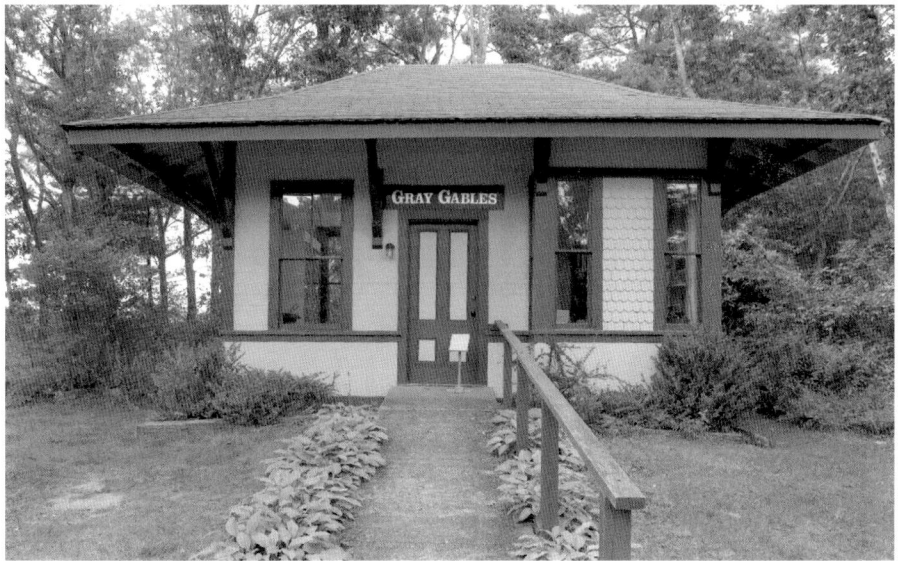

The Gray Gables train depot. *Courtesy of the* Cape Cod Times.

wife was the youngest first lady in U.S. history. The couple wanted a summer house where they could bring their growing family for fun and relaxation. Cleveland liked to travel around town in a battered fedora and fishing boots.

Many memorable events happened here for Cleveland in Gray Gables. Along with victory parties (he was the only president to serve two non-consecutive terms, from 1885 to 1889 and from 1893 to 1897), he received word of his second presidential nomination there in June 1892. His son Francis was born there in 1903. Also, unbeknownst to the outside world, Cleveland had a malignant growth on the roof of his mouth removed on the yacht of his friend, Commodore E.C. Benedict. Then, tragedy struck. His oldest daughter, Ruth, died of diphtheria during the winter of 1904, after which Cleveland lost interest in Gray Gables. After serving out his presidential term, Cleveland retired to Princeton, New Jersey, and died in 1908.

Gray Gables was leased in the summer of 1904 and then sold. In a later era, the building became an inn, but it was destroyed by fire in 1973. According to the Bourne Historical Society, Cleveland's personal train station was a flag stop, used by Cataumet and Pocasset students to travel to Bourne High School. It was moved to the Aptucxet Trading Post Museum in 1976.

NANTUCKET'S PRESIDENTIAL CONNECTIONS

Nantucket, too, was a popular place for presidents to visit. We often think of Martha's Vineyard and Hyannis Port as presidential hotspots, but Nantucket can claim some presidential glamour as well.

During the nineteenth century, Nantucket saw many presidential visits. For example, Ulysses S. Grant stayed at the Ocean House (now the Jared Coffin House) in 1874. Chester Arthur lunched on the island with Henry A. Willard, who built the Willard Hotel in Washington, D.C., in 1882. Also, Benjamin Harrison visited in 1890. Last but not least, Grover Cleveland made a day trip from his summer home in Gray Gables.

The twentieth century also saw its share of visiting presidents. Woodrow Wilson made a private visit in 1917 to see his daughter in Siasconset. Later, in 1933, Franklin Delano Roosevelt sailed the *Amberjack II* into Nantucket Harbor from Rhode Island, but due to a storm, he never made it to shore. John F. Kennedy also sailed over in 1963 but didn't come ashore. President Bill Clinton—who made four trips to the island between 1999 and 2006—was the first to arrive on the island on *Air Force One*. In an interesting twist, Bill Clinton and George H.W. Bush visited the island within four days of each other (August 14–17, 2005). It was also an annual tradition for former vice president Joe Biden and his family to spend Thanksgivings on the island.

These whirlwind political stops were often accompanied by tourist enthusiasm and security headaches. As long as people enjoy vacationing on the Cape and the Islands, U.S. presidents are sure to stop by for their dose of sun, surf and summertime pursuits.

MARTHA'S VINEYARD AS A PRESIDENTIAL VACATION MECCA

Serving as president of the United States is a noble yet arduous position, so it comes as no surprise that not just one but two recent presidents have spent their summer vacations on Martha's Vineyard. First, President Bill Clinton arrived in 1993 along with his wife, Hillary, and daughter, Chelsea, the first year of his presidency, and made several other trips there as well. The first family stayed with their longtime friend Richard L. Friedman in 1994 and from 1997 through 2000. From leisurely bike rides to sunning on the beach, golfing and visiting favorite restaurants and bookstores, the Clintons enjoyed

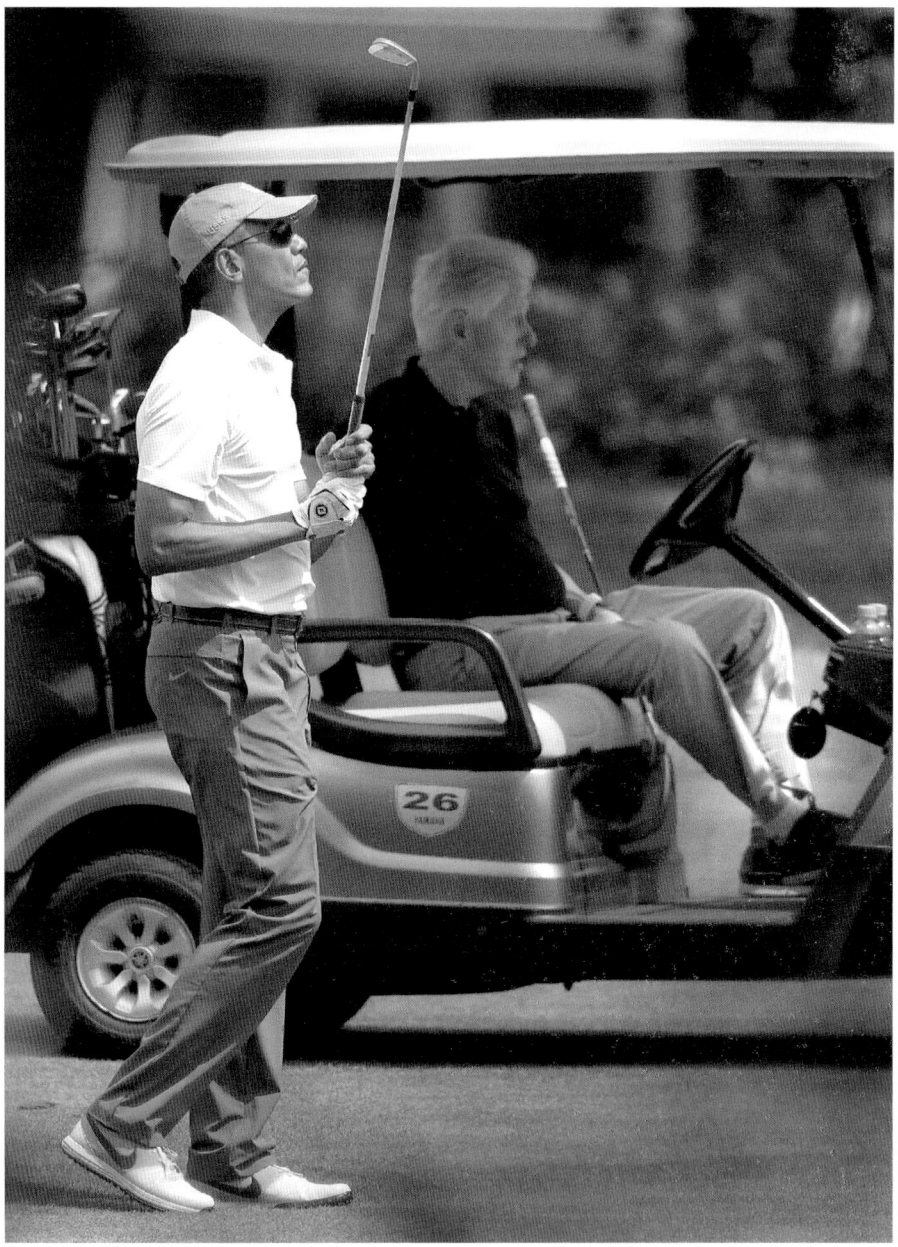

Presidents Barack Obama and Bill Clinton playing golf on Martha's Vineyard. *Courtesy of the* Cape Cod Times.

the island lifestyle. A favorite spot for golfing was Farm Neck Golf Club, the only eighteen-hole golf course on the island. There were sailing trips with Jackie Onassis aboard the *Relemar* and swimming and sailing with Ted Kennedy. They dined with celebrities like Jimmy Buffett, William Styron and Carly Simon. There were also high-profile events with Bill Gates and Sylvester Stallone.

In late August 2009, Barack Obama and his family took their first island vacation. They stayed at the Blue Heron Farm, a twenty-eight-acre waterfront estate. The president enjoyed golfing and reading; in fact, local news outlets always printed a list of notable books President Obama set aside to read during his vacation. The Obamas spent every vacation on the Vineyard except for 2012, when the president was running for reelection. These visits were more low-key than the Clintons, when, as reported in the *Boston Globe*, the Obamas would have a "romantic dinner at the Beach Plum Inn, slurp ice cream cones at Mad Martha's, and bike at water's edge."

The added security often overtaxed the island community, but there was the added boost to the economy as well-wishers followed both the Clintons and the Obamas in hopes of getting a snapshot or a handshake.

George H.W. Bush Visits Mashpee

One visit from a sitting president occurred for more political reasons. On the morning of November 1, 1990, President George H.W. Bush stopped in Mashpee on a whirlwind trip through Massachusetts. He was stumping for the election of William Weld for governor and John Rappaport for the U.S. Senate. Prior to his visit, Old Barnstable Road had its center line painted red, white and blue in honor of Bush's stopover in Mashpee.

According to a *Cape Cod Times* article, during his brief visit at the Mashpee Middle School, Bush told his audience, "Let me say how great it is to be back on the Cape, to breathe the deep magic of this place. You know, Henry David Thoreau, Massachusetts' native son, once said about the Cape: 'A man may stand here and put all America behind him.' Way back in 1943, in the fall, just about this time in 1943, I spent some time at the Cape, stationed at the naval air station, then at Hyannis. I've never forgotten the joy and the wonder of the Cape. It's great to be back." Whether they agreed with his politics, the citizens of Mashpee were proud to host a president if only for a day.

PATTI PAGE

THE CONTINUING ALLURE OF "OLD CAPE COD"

Patti Page, America's songbird and a top-selling female singer in the 1950s, made Cape Cod famous when she released the song "Old Cape Cod" in June 1957 on Mercury Records. Clara Ann Fowler was born on November 8, 1927, in Claremore, Oklahoma, into a large family so poor that they went without electricity. She also picked cotton along with her mother and sisters. After graduating from high school in 1945, she started her career as a singer with Al Clauser and his Oklahoma Outlaws at KTUL radio station and became a feature singer in a fifteen-minute radio show at age eighteen. Since the show was sponsored by the Page Milk Company, the young singer became known as "Patti Page." She was later discovered by Jack Rael, a saxophone player, after he heard her radio show and asked her to join his band. He would later become her personal manager.

Her first hit single was "Confess" in 1947. Her first million-selling hit was "With My Eyes Wide Open, I'm Dreaming." One of her most popular songs was her version of the "Tennessee Waltz," which came out in 1950. She was a forerunner in that she overdubbed her vocals when she couldn't afford to hire backup singers. "Old Cape Cod" was written by Claire Rothrock, Milton Yakus and Allan Jeffrey in 1957. When she recorded the song, Patti Page had never visited Cape Cod. Cape Codders immediately fell in love with the song and coined it the "unofficial Cape Cod anthem." In fact, many people felt the song helped to put Cape Cod on the map.

The song has sensuous lyrics that start out: "If you're fond of sand dunes and salty air/Quaint little villages here and there/ You're sure to fall in

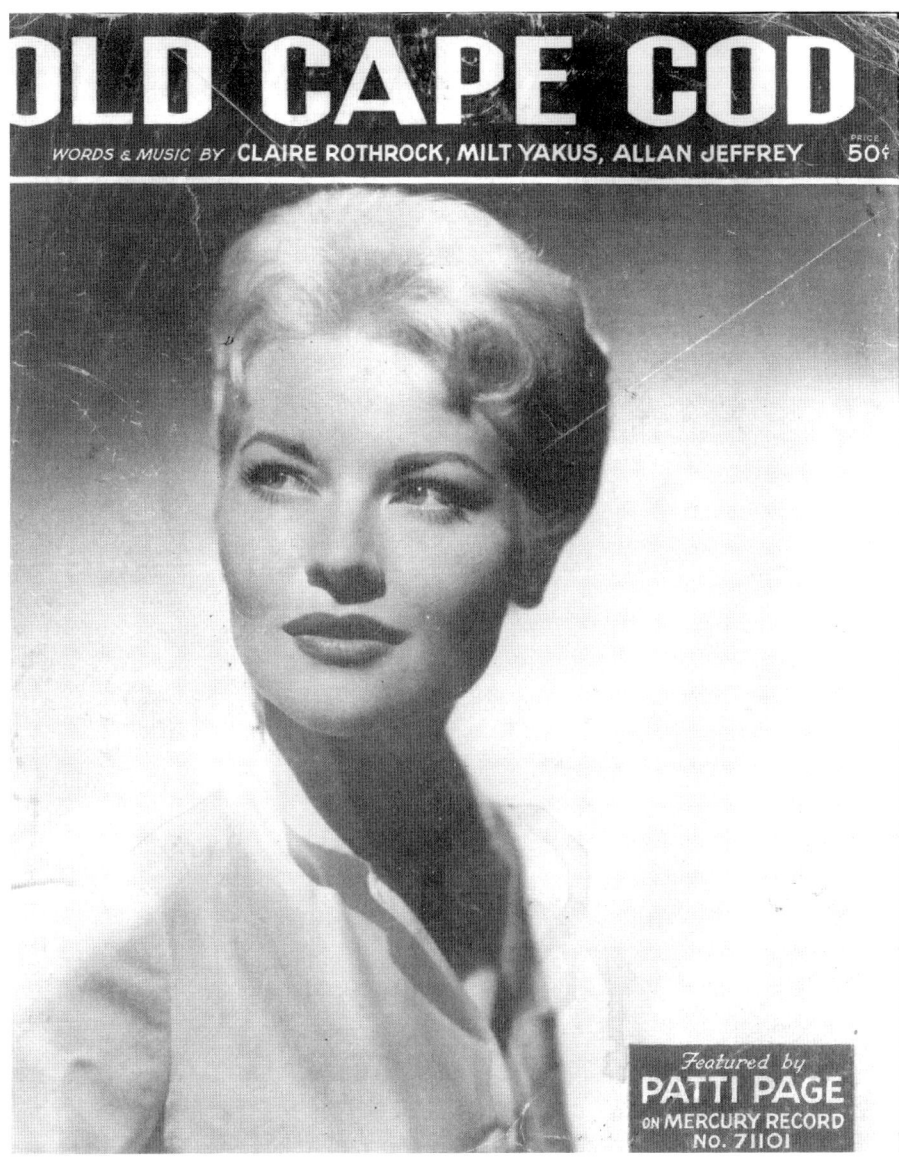

The sheet music cover for "Old Cape Cod," sung by Patti Page. *From the sheet music collection of Gregory R. Johnson.*

love with old Cape Cod." In 2010, Page visited Cape Cod to promote her memoir *This Is My Song.* The Cape Cod Chamber of Commerce changed its street name to "Patti Page Way" in her honor. A 2010 *Cape Cod Times* article described Page's reaction when she finally visited the Cape: "I could not believe it when I finally did go, because I realized that [the song] had captured something about a place that I had had within me for so many years, but never knew. It's unexplainable to me, because it's so dear to me—I knew I had been here before [although] I hadn't."

Patti Page died at age eighty-five on January 1, 2013, in Encinitas, California. Her legacy lives on through the lyrics that have brought Cape Cod to life for so many residents and visitors.

A CAPE COD CHILDHOOD

Off-Cape residents often ask what it's like to live on Cape Cod year-round. This has always struck me as an odd question. My reply would be, "We do the same things you do at home." In other words, life here is a daily round of familiar scenes and experiences. However, my childhood was a uniquely Cape experience.

My parents moved our family to Cape Cod in the early 1960s from Lansdale, Pennsylvania. My father hoped to start an art gallery of his paintings, so my parents bought a two-story Cape in the town of Orleans. I loved the place from the moment we arrived. Unlike the "ticky-tacky" development of identical houses that we'd left behind, we moved to a beautiful house with a salt marsh across the road and a large field next to our house. I had never known such freedom to roam.

From exploring the beaches in summer and collecting shells on the long sandy flats of Skaket Beach to biking down to Rock Harbor, we were always on the go. My sisters and I loved the outdoors and would spend long hours playing in our grassy backyard. Some evenings I would venture out with my next-door neighbor and her mother to meet the fishing boats at Rock Harbor. My friend's father was a fisherman and would bring home his day's wages for the family's money jar. It was exciting to watch the boats come in, feel the wind on my face and hear the screech of seagulls as they circled the harbor.

We were quite isolated and had little access to shopping centers or other urban outlets. Twice a year we would travel the mid-Cape highway to

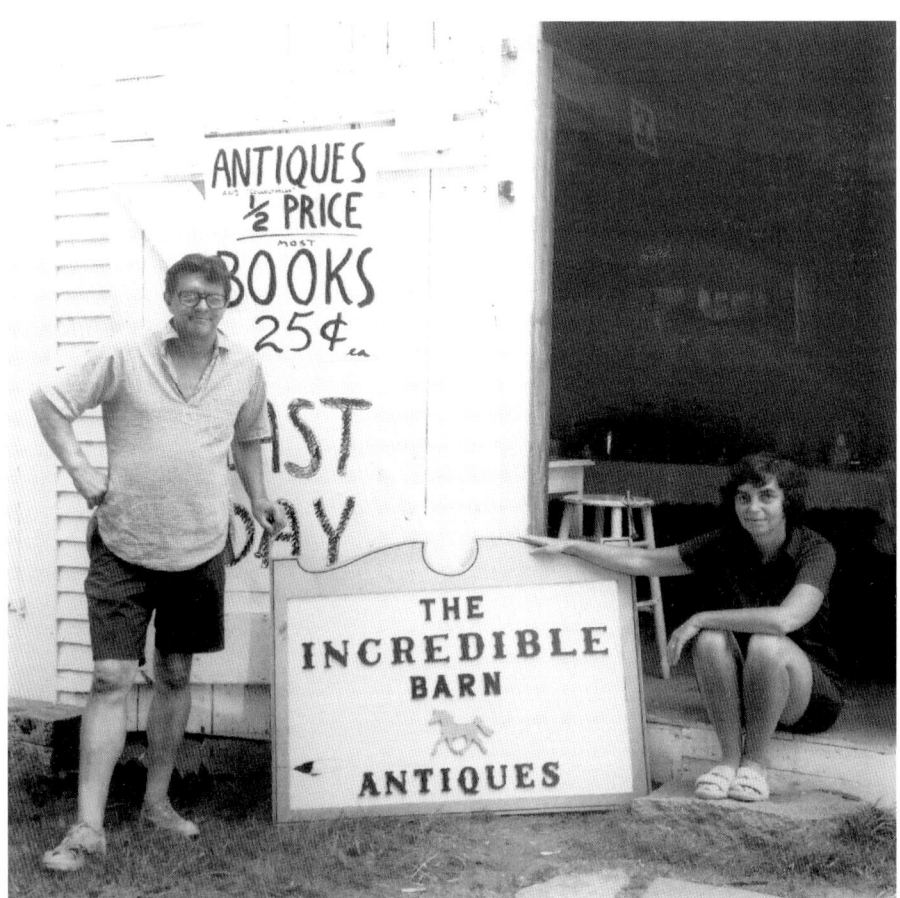

Photo of Muriel and Wendell Smith in front of their antique and book shop, the Incredible Barn, in East Orleans, circa 1972. *From the collection of Dell and Liz Smith.*

Kings or Zayre's in Hyannis for back-to-school and Christmas shopping. This was a big event in our lives, and we always had our lists ready for the trip. In summer, we had swimming lessons at Pleasant Bay in South Orleans and met a family from New Jersey there who became lasting friends. At this time, my father taught English at Sea Pines School in Brewster, so we had our Sunday dinners at the school. Later, we moved to Main Street in East Orleans, where my parents started their antiques and bookshop, the Incredible Barn. I acquired my love for oddments and antiques from helping my parents in their store.

The year I turned thirteen, my mother brought home a mannequin to use for modeling antique clothing. She let me name her (Cordelia) and brought me along on buying trips so I could help choose her dresses since we wore the same size. A year or two later, Cordelia was sold to the artist Robert Vickrey to use as a scarecrow for his dock on Crystal Lake. That winter, she floated away in a storm and was discovered by a passerby who thought she was a drowning victim. So much for the fate of poor Cordelia.

These are happy memories. I loved growing up on Cape Cod with the ocean in my backyard. Tennessee Williams once said, "Home is where you hang your childhood."

BIBLIOGRAPHY

The Cape Cod Times *was originally part of the* New Bedford Standard Times *and called the* Cape Cod Standard Times. *When the newspaper became its own entity in 1974, the name was changed to the* Cape Cod Times.

Barnouw, Erik. *A History of Broadcasting.* New York: Oxford University Press, 1996–70.

Beston, Henry. *The Outermost House: A Year of Life on the Great Beach of Cape Cod.* New York: Ballantine Books, 1928.

Chamberlain, Samuel. *Cape Cod in the Sun.* New York: Hastings House, 1937.

Damore, Leo. *In His Garden.* New York: Random House, 1990.

Del Deo, Josephine. *Figures in a Landscape: The Life and Times of the American Painter, Ross Moffett, 1888–1971.* Virginia Beach, VA: Donning Company, 1994.

Gordon, Dan, and Gary Joseph. *Cape Encounters: Contemporary Cape Cod Ghost Stories.* Hyannis, MA: Cockle Cove Press, 2004.

Green, Eugene, William Sachese and Brian McCauley. *The Names of Cape Cod.* Wellesley, MA: Acadia Press, 2006.

Jasper, Mark. *Haunted Inns of New England.* North Attleborough, MA: Covered Bridge Press, 2000.

Klim, Jake. *Attack on Orleans: The World War I Submarine Raid on Cape Cod.* Charleston, SC: The History Press, 2014.

Lawson, Evelyn. *Yesterday's Cape Cod.* Miami, FL: E.A. Seemann Pub., 1975.

Lombardo, Daniel. *Orleans.* Charleston, SC: Arcadia Publishing, 2001.

Maloney, Joan M. *Harwich*. Charleston, SC: Arcadia Publishing, 2001.

Nickerson, Joseph A., and Geraldine D. Nickerson. *Chatham Sea Captains in the Age of Sail*. Charleston, SC: The History Press, 2008.

O'Connell, James C. *Becoming Cape Cod: Creating a Seaside Resort*. Hanover, NH: University Press of New England, 2003.

Quinn, William. *Shipwrecks Around Cape Cod*. Farmington, ME: Knowlton & McLeary, 1973.

Rex, Percy Fielitz. *The Prolific Pencil: A Biography of Joseph Crosby Lincoln*. Taunton, MA: W.S. Sullwold Pub., 1980.

Sabbag, Robert. *Down Around Midnight: A Memoir of Crash and Survival*. New York: Viking, 2009.

Seufert, Christopher. *In the Footsteps of Marconi*. Chatham, MA: Christopher Seufert Photography, 2010.

Snow, Edward Rowe. *Storms and Shipwrecks of New England*. Beverly, MA: Commonwealth Editions, 2003.

Stone, Dr. Thomas Newcomb. *Cape Cod Rhymes*. Cambridge, MA: Riverside Press, 1896.

Vuilleumier, Marion. *Earning a Living on Olde Cape Cod*. Craigville, MA: Craigville Press, 1968.

Newspapers and Magazines

Associated Press.
Boston Globe.
Boston Herald Traveler.
Boston Irish Reporter.
Cape Cod Colonial.
Cape Cod Guide.
Cape Cod Life Magazine.
Cape Cod Standard Times.
Cape Cod Times.
New Bedford Standard Times.
New York Post.
New York Times.
Patriot Ledger.
Provincetown Advocate.
(Yarmouth) Register Newspaper.

Other Resources

Bourne Historical Society, Buzzards Bay, Massachusetts.

Cape Cod Canal Region Chamber of Commerce, Buzzards Bay, Massachusetts. http://www.capecodcanalchamber.org.

The Cape Cod Five Cents Savings Bank. www.capecodfive.com.

The Cataumet Schoolhouse. www.cataumetschoolhouse.org.

Chatham Historical Society. www.chathamhistoricalsociety.org.

Discover Nantucket. blog.discovernantucket.com.

The Edward Gorey House. www.edwardgoreyhouse.org.

Famous Scientists. www.famousscientists.org.

George H.W. Bush Public Papers. bushlibrary.tamu.edu.

A Gothic Curiosity Cabinet. www.gothichorrorstories.com.

Historic Massachusetts. This is a pictorial travel map published in the '50s and '60s.

Hyannis Public Library. www.hyannislibrary.org.

The Internet Movie Database. www.imdb.com.

Legend Tripping. www.legendtripping.com.

Mass Home. www.masshome.com.

National Transportation Safety Board.

Native Languages of the Americas. www.native-languages.com.

New England Historical Society. http://www.newenglandhistoricalsociety.com.

Paranormal Encounters. www.paranormal-encounters.com.

Plimoth Plantation. www.plimoth.org.

Popular Mechanics. www.popularmechanics.com.

Sandwich Glass Museum. www.sandwichglassmuseum.org.

Sandwich Historical Society. www.sandwichhistorical.org.

Sandwich Monthly Meeting. capecodquakers.org.

Smithsonian Archives of American Art. https://www.aaa.si.edu.

Town of Eastham, Massachusetts. www.eastham-ma.gov.

U.S. Army Corps of Engineers, New England District. http://www.nae.usace.army.mil.

Wychmere Beach Club. wychmerebeachclub.com.

INDEX

ABOUT THE AUTHOR

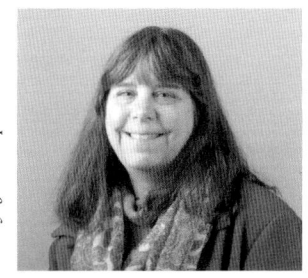

Robin Smith-Johnson grew up in Orleans, Massachusetts, where she honed her love of reading and creative writing. She has degrees in English from Wheaton College in Norton, Massachusetts, and Bowling Green State University in Ohio. She is the former newsroom librarian at the *Cape Cod Times* and currently teaches in the English Department at Cape Cod Community College. She is the author of two books of poetry, as well as *Legends and Lore of Cape Cod* from The History Press. Robin lives in Mashpee, Massachusetts, with her family.